"A fresh and exciting addition to the literature on the Beatitudes."

—Dr. CARL BATES, Pastor, First Baptist Church, Charlotte, North Carolina

"Develops the inner meaning of the Sermon on the Mount's precious but concise statements from our Lord . . ."

—Dr. HUBER DRUMWRIGHT, Dean, School of Theology, Southwestern Baptist Theological Seminary, Fort Worth, Texas

"Allen is a craftsman with words . . . graphic illustrations . . . the depth of Christ's message . . ."

—JOHN J. HURT, Editor, *The Baptist Standard*, Dallas, Texas

DIVINE DIVIDENDS

DIVINE DIVIDENDS

An Inspirational Reading
of the Sermon on the Mount

R. Earl Allen

THOMAS NELSON INC.
NASHVILLE / NEW YORK

Library of Congress Cataloging in Publication Data

Allen, R   Earl.
  Divine Dividends; an inspirational reading of the
Sermon on the mount.

  1. Beatitudes—Sermons. 2. Baptists—Sermons.
3. Sermons, American. I. Title.
BT382.A42   226'.93'066   74–4474
ISBN 0–8407–5564–3

*This book is
dedicated to my
fellow members who
minister unto me*

Dr. M. C. McCarroll

Dr. Roger W. Moore

Dr. J. H. Horn

Contents

Foreword

Take Jesus as the greatest of all preachers in His *Sermon On The Mount*. Center attention in the Beatitudes and to the central truth of each verse add an application for our time. The result is *Divine Dividends,* and the best in R. Earl Allen as preacher, teacher and author.

Don't label *Divine Dividends* as a book of sermons. It is that, but it is more for Allen is a craftsman with words and the preaching takes the form of a narrative, capturing attention and holding it.

Don't label *Divine Dividends* as a book of devotionals. The connotation doesn't allow for the depth of Christ's message which Allen explores and develops from every verse.

Graphic illustrations punctuate the author's message in each chapter. His skillful play on words, such as "The Might of the Meek" and "The Mystery of Mercy" in chapter titles, attracts attention and leads the reader from one chapter into the next.

*Divine Dividend*s is R. Earl Allen at his best. That commends this latest in his prolific preaching and teaching through the printed page.

JOHN J. HURT, Editor
The Baptist Standard

DIVINE
DIVIDENDS

Blessed are the poor in spirit

Chapter 1

The Life to Live

The place where Jesus preached the Sermon on the Mount is one of the few places in what is called "The Holy Land" that remains as it was during Jesus' time. From the hillside, a very large, sloping area, the Sea of Galilee is visible. It seemed to be one of the Lord's favorite locales.

The message of the Master recorded in the fifth, sixth, and seventh chapters of Matthew, called the Sermon on the Mount, would take about twenty-two minutes to read. But it would take a lifetime to comprehend it. Jesus perhaps spent the entire night in prayer before giving this message.

Also, it is believed that the time was about the halfway mark in Jesus' public ministry. His popularity was evidently at its peak. He seemed to be shifting emphasis. He meant for His followers to consider the Kingdom here as well as the Kingdom hereafter and He began to describe the Kingdom-men. "And seeing the multitudes, he went up into a mountain: and when he was set, his disciples came unto him: And he opened his mouth, and taught them, saying, Blessed are the poor in spirit: for theirs is the kingdom of heaven [God]" (Matthew 5:1–3).

The salesman knows that his opening words are crucial. He polishes his "pitch" to perfection. Jesus was a master of communication.

Surely the audience, His disciples and followers, the critics and curiosity seekers, sat spellbound by His opening words. The crowd may have extended to the very top of the mountain. It was said on another occasion, "Never man spoke like this man!"

On no other occasion did Jesus speak like He spoke on this occasion. His reputation had labeled Him more a "wonder-worker" than an orator. But no words have ever been so widely quoted, so greatly revered, yet so consistently evaded as these words of Jesus. We have memorized them and mouthed them from time to time, but we rarely accept and practice them as being real and basic—something you can "put your teeth into." We do not take them as relevant to our lives in the age in which we live. We tend to think, "Well, that was back in Jesus' time," and that by the standards of today's society they make little sense.

These pronouncements contradicted popular thinking

and acknowledged the unpleasant realities of life. The rich were getting richer and the poor were getting poorer. "Blessed are the poor"? Some of them shuddered when they thought of such a thing. But this word "blessed" brings out a problem of semantics.

Perhaps the best translation into present-day language would be the word "happy." Yet I do not really like to use that word because we are on a "happy kick" in America just now. We ask of everything we do, "Will this make me happy?" We rarely question, "Will it make me strong? Will it make me consistent? Will it build my character? Will it help somebody?" Selfishly we demand, "Will this make us happy?" The origin of the word "happy" comes from the old English word "hap," which means "can it happen so?"

But "blessed" is not something that just happens. Jesus was implying inner peace and joy: "more happy is that man." It does not do violence to the original to put it, "Congratulations! More secure is the man who feels this way. Blessed is the man who has come to such a place in his life."

In writing the Declaration of Independence, Thomas Jefferson talked about the "right to life, liberty, and the pursuit of happiness." That is something America has been pursuing ever since. But this concept came out of the English law which reads, "the pursuit of property." Even though home-ownership is one of those things all of us desire, Jefferson recognized that property in itself did not guarantee happiness, so he revised it to the "pursuit of happiness." We are all pursuing the same thing, but Jesus' words rebuked prevailing attitudes of selfishness, greediness, and obsessive ambition.

The word "blessed" is familiar to us, but we hear it at church more than we hear it anywhere else. It's not the king of word we use in the grocery store, in the business world, or on the playground. It has a saccharine-sweet sound that is somehow not very meaningful to us.

What did Jesus first call "blessed"?

A Puzzling Revelation

At first appearance, the words "Blessed are the poor in spirit" are *a puzzling revelation*, especially when we realize that the word "blessed" would better be translated "happy." What did Jesus mean?

In the language of His day, there were two words that could be translated "poor." One word meant barely making a living, just getting by, only a little under-nourished. Another word meant absolute poverty, and it was used of the beggar Lazarus. That is the word Jesus used in this verse. It got their attention, for He was speaking to mostly poor people who scarcely knew where their next meal was coming from. In that day the land of Palestine would have qualified for a poverty program.

"Blessed are the poor in spirit," He said. Jesus taught in absolutes, and I do not know how to deal with His absolutes except to approach the concept in a negative way. Maybe by comparisons we can get the picture.

Certainly He was not extolling spinelessness. He was

not saying that His people should be cringing, spiritless, lacking in backbone. He demanded "soldiers of the Cross." Everything He did and said was inconsistent with namby-pamby pictures of Him some artists have painted.

One Greek philosopher of Plato's day lived in a barrel. He took great pride in his "poverty" and rebuked Plato harshly for living in a house and having a chariot. But even pride in humility was included in Jesus' declaration —pride of any kind!

Let us be careful to understand what it means, in spiritual terms, to be poor and to be rich. Again, we are dealing with language which is imprecise and heavily loaded with connotations. The poor in spirit are not those who overplay their humble bit: "I'm nobody!" Those are self-pitying people who run themselves down, criticize their own ineffectiveness, and cringe at the smallest slight.

Such an individual we find pictured in the New Testament parable of the talents—the man with one talent. "Other people are making it better than I am," he thought, "and even my master is dealing harshly with me. I knew he was a hard man, and I didn't bother to try. I'm a nobody!"

Similarly, too many Christians say, "Surely God isn't going to expect me to be responsible for using this poor little talent that I have!"

Small things in themselves are not necessarily little or unimportant. This was not true of the "widow's mite"— about two pennies. It is not true about any part of life. But we can let ourselves become little in spirit: childish, selfish, and dwarfed.

The spies Moses sent to look at Canaan had the same problem—they were spiritless and faithless men. They looked over the fertile land, saw the huge warriors, and came back depressed. They forgot the greatness of God, the promises of God, the loving-kindness of God. They came back and gave their report: "The inhabitants look like giants! We were as grasshoppers in their sight!"

In the New Testament, a Pharisee and a publican went into the temple to pray. The Pharisee, self-inflated and proud, raised himself as if on elevated shoes: "I thank God that I'm not like other men!" Over to the side, in an inconspicuous place, the publican prayed, "Lord, have mercy on me, a sinner!" It is not difficult to distinguish which one was poor in spirit. The Pharisee lusted for fame and the praise of men. It's not a perfect translation, but not altogether inaccurate, if we use the phrase "poor sport" of the man who will not humble himself.

In the story of the prodigal son, we find the example of the elder brother, who lived with riches all about him and a great supply of fatted calves to be killed. But this elder son exhibited a jealous spirit and refused to attend his brother's homecoming feast.

What kind of spirit do we have toward our brethren, toward our fellow man, toward the world? One who has a normal attitude toward himself usually has about the same attitude toward other people. If he has a high sense of values, then he usually places high value on other people. If everything is cheap to him, everybody else usually seems cheap, also.

A Difficult Reality

What is Jesus saying through this beatitude to us, who live two thousand years later? Certainly to be poor in spirit in our "affluent society" is *a difficult reality*. In our quest for material things, we often become victims of our environment.

Kierkegaard told of watching wild ducks flying through at migration time. They lighted on a farm pond where a farmer was throwing out corn for tame ducks. This was an easier life than they had been used to. When the flock flew on, one remained, picking up corn. Months went by. When the season was over and the ducks flew back south with the passing of warmth, this duck spread his wings to fly and found that he could no longer leave the ground. He had become a commodity for the farmer's table—a victim of his environment. His stomach had outdistanced his wings!

One of the greatest dangers in your lives is your environment. Or rather, how you meet your environment. How you live, how you involve yourself, and the values you place on others or on yourself—they may be misplaced values. The only true values are the spiritual riches of God. On the positive side, to be "poor in spirit" is to know oneself to be spiritually impoverished, unable to supply our own spiritual needs.

Moses was a mighty man in the Old Testament, but the

Bible says he was a meek man. He was "poor in spirit". He felt he was inadequate to the task to which God called him. "O God," he pled, "how can I go to Pharaoh and say, 'Let my people go!'?"

God's answer was, "I will go with thee."

This poverty of spirit is what we ought to feel as we come to worship. The prophet Isaiah did. In the sixth chapter, he "saw the Lord high and lifted up," and cried out. "Woe is me, for I am undone, because I am a man of unclean lips, and I dwell in the midst of a people of unclean lips; for mine eyes have seen the King, the Lord of hosts" (Isaiah 6:5). That was poverty of spirit.

We may appear prosperous, we may dress well, we may seem healthy and happy, but Jesus was talking about spiritual things. Down inside our hearts, where God speaks and God walks, He knows our thoughts. When we realize this, we have to join Isaiah in confessing ,"O God, I am uncovered before Thee. Thou knowest my poverty, my emptiness, my nothingness!" God can use a man like that! In fact, it is not long before a man like that *wants* to be used. Isaiah said, "Here am I, send me!"

People who wish not to be used are self-inflated people. They feel they are too important for the lowly tasks. They raise themselves above the level of the rest of their church, saying they must offer themselves to a wider area of service. God help them! For if we become victims of our environment, accepting the values of this world, we lose the consciousness that deep down we are poverty-stricken before God. We feel we can do it on our own, we don't need God.

The word "poor" here implies such complete poverty that it forces a man to be a beggar. Such a man cannot be a "know-it-all" but begs for God's strength, guidance, and wisdom. Many so-called Christian leaders need to come to the humility of Gideon, a humble layman to whom God spoke in Old Testament days. "Gideon, I need you," God called.

"Lord, You can't use me!" Gideon replied. "Behold, my family is poor in Manasseh, and I am the least in my father's house" (Judges 6:15). But as soon as God convinced Gideon He could use him, he answered, "Lord, here am I." He didn't make excuses: "Use me, Lord!"

Once, in poverty of spirit, Simon Peter said, "Depart from me; for I am a sinful man, O Lord" (Luke 5:8). Later, Peter told his Master, "I don't care how many others may forsake You, but Lord, You can put it down that *I* will never leave You!"

The next morning, when the cock crowed, tears came to Peter's eyes as he realized he had denied his Lord. It was a dark morning for Simon Peter. He had to say to his Risen Lord, "I am not a worthy tabernacle in which You could live. Lord, You saw me in my shame and my sin, and You heard my cursing and my lying." Peter felt very unworthy, very poor in spirit: "O God, You can't use me; I have played the fool!"

Another instance where humility gave way to haughtiness was in the life of the man who became Israel's first king. We first hear of young Saul tending his father's herds. But when the people sought him to make him king, he was hiding in the baggage. Later, a sad time came when, in arrogance, Saul took upon himself the role of the priest. After he had become king, he began to feel that he owned the whole country and the temple of God, too.

Samuel, the anointed priest of God, walked in and rebuked the king, telling Saul he was rejected by God. Later on, Samuel reminded the puffed-up king of his early humility. "When thou wast little in thine own sight, wast thou not made . . . king over Israel?" (1 Samuel 15:17). Back there, Saul had been big in the sight of the people and little in his own sight. But he came to the place where he was little in the sight of the people and big in his own sight.

Are there any Sauls among us? God has been gracious and good, but we have strutted and strayed, felt that we were sharper and luckier than others, that we could leave God out.

A rich young ruler came to Jesus. "Good Master," he said, "what must I do to inherit the Kingdom of God?"

"If thou wilt be perfect, go and sell what thou hast," Jesus replied, "and come and follow me" (Matthew 19:21).

The rich young man went away sorrowfully, not because he could not be saved, being rich, but because he trusted in his riches and thought that they should buy his way. You remember that Jesus said, "*I* am the door" (John 10:9), and "I am the way, the truth, and the life" (John 14:6). You can't crash the door, you don't buy the gate, if you please, to come to Jesus. No man's riches avail.

"Blessed are the poor in spirit." Jesus was also saying, "Blessed is that man who is not possessed by his possessions."

The word used in the Greek language which means humility also means meekness. These meanings overlap, but each carries a different shade that is necessary to being out the total idea Jesus was expressing. M. R. Vincent said of this word: "Another word which, though never used in a bad sense, has been lifted to a higher plane by Christianity and made the symbol of a higher good."

Nobody wanted to be humble before Jesus came and showed the way. Pride, power, possessions . . . these were the great goals of life. To the pagan, humility meant "condescension," but Jesus gave it a different meaning. Rather than "putting up with," it became to the Christian, "willing submission to the Lord's will." In a sense, Jesus coined a new word for new men. He lifted out the idea and gave it new meaning.

Humility is the capstone of spiritual achievement, said the Lord. It was something Jesus' listeners didn't know anything about, but He made it a crowning virtue. Our lives contain much that is counterfeit, but we cannot counterfeit humility. Our problem is, perhaps, that in mass production we turn out poor copies of the pattern. But blessed is the man who follows Jesus' pattern of humility, who is "poor in spirit."

I'm not always sure just what humility is, outworking in everyday life, but I'm sure I know what humility isn't. I flew to a West Texas city for a funeral in a nearby town. Time was pressing. The winds had made the plane at least twenty minutes late and I had to be driven 55 miles after reaching the airport. At sixty minutes until time for the funeral, we landed. Sitting on the airport side, I saw them begin to roll out the red carpet, and I knew it wasn't for me. "It will be a twenty-minute wait for all passengers," the stewardess said.

"Lady," I insisted, "I must get off this plane. I have a funeral to conduct. I need to get off before the ceremonies."

The well-known young man for whom the reception was being prepared was sitting across the aisle. He spoke up. "Please let him off," he said. And they did. I went down the red carpet—it was already there, I had to. I stepped off quickly as I could. One of my friends, waiting for me, saw my unscheduled exit and raised his eyebrows.

"Pat Boone said to leave it out there for him, too," I quipped to the startled master of ceremonies. I'm afraid that wasn't humility. But the young man had the right spirit, not holding up somebody in need, that he might have pre-eminence. He didn't lose a thing. In fact, he gained a great deal in the sight of many people.

A Privileged Reward

Poverty of spirit—but that's just half of it! "Blessed are the poor in spirit: for theirs is the kingdom of God." We hear the Lord speaking of *a privileged reward*—the kingdom of God.

In the rush of the world today, we don't want even "pie in the sky by and by." We don't want to wait, we want it now! However, Christians should be happy now, for theirs *is* the Kingdom of God—they possess it already.

Jesus was not making a promise, but talking about an end result. It was a statement of present possession. Blessed *are* those who have this spirit, for no man can be happy until he simply comes and says, "Lord, I'm not worthy, I have nothing. I can only give myself to You. Thank You, God. Amen!"

Now, that's the beginning. The kingdom of God within grows toward a final perfection and future reality.

Jesus' words built upon a promise of God in the Old Testament: "All those things hath mine hand made, . . . saith the Lord; but to this man will I look, even to him that is poor and of a contrite spirit and trembleth at my word" (Isaiah 66:2).

This first is the basic beatitude; this is the foundation, the beginning of them all. A man has to empty himself so that he can be filled with the characteristics of the Christian: I am nothing, I have nothing. As the old gospel song puts it:

27

Nothing in my hand I bring;
Simply to Thy cross I cling.

Is this relevant in our time? Is it not pertinent for the
problems of our day? Becoming "poor in spirit" is not
losing reality like with LSD, but coming face to face
with reality and recognizing that things of this world offer no hope, no peace.

Jesus was leaving the flatlands of spiritual achievement
and going toward the mountains, traveling without luggage. Happy is that man who doesn't trust in his possessions; happy is that man who doesn't depend upon the
things of this world; happy is that man who has within
him peace with God and confidence in God. The future
is not for the haughty, but for the humble. Blessed is that
man who possesses the kingdom of God and has the joy
of Christ in his heart.

John D. Rockefeller, Sr., one of the richest men on
earth in his time, said that "There never is a man as poor
as the man who has nothing but money."

Jesus was the Great Physician; He knew the cure for
all ills. He was the greatest psychologist and psychiatrist
ever known. The beatitudes offer a basis for stable life-
adjustment. Before physicians used a couch, He recognized the value of a man unburdening himself to a trusted
friend. "Confess your faults one to another," He in-
structed. Of course, today we have become so friendless
that we have to turn it over to the professionals. We
cannot trust our friends.

Jesus, in giving this first beatitude, was removing the ego. The God who made mankind, the God-man, Himself, was taking away the great "capital I" in man, getting it out of the way. It blocks the blessings God has in store for us.

This beatitude is a prescription for the dethronement of pride. When we lose the self-importance of "I" and fall on our knees—whether it is in rededication, reconsecration to our task, or coming to the Lord in salvation —we have not only found God, but we have found ourselves. Life becomes worth living in the Kingdom of God.

Blessed are they that mourn

Chapter 2

Solace in Sorrow

What remarkable words to fall from the lips of Jesus Christ: "Blessed are they that mourn"! And this concept presented by Christ can be attained by no man unless he first accepts the plan of salvation provided by Christ.

In Matthew 5, Jesus was speaking of the charter of Christian life, the standards of His Kingdom.

The second Beatitude says, in full, "Blessed are they that mourn; for they *shall* be comforted" (Matthew 5:4). It follows logically after the first, for surely those who are "poor in spirit"—tender and submissive toward God— will mourn over all that grieves God.

The entire Sermon on the Mount, of which these beatitudes are a part, describes the Christian's heritage. How many religions on the face of the earth can say, "I believe in all that"? These are not platitudes, but deeply challenging statements. In fact, when these principles from God's Word are stressed, they may bring real conflict into our lives.

When people feel a preacher has "quit preaching and gone to meddling," they often complain, "I wish that preacher would just stick to the simple Sermon on the Mount. That's good enough for me!" Those who say that do not realize that there is nothing simple about the Sermon on the Mount. It contains some of the most profound philosophy in the Bible. We too often become used to scanning the familiar verses in a hurry, not noticing that they make some arresting statements that challenge our lives.

This beatitude throws the light of God's blessing on an unpleasant human condition: having to do without what the world values so highly, peace and prosperity.

Jesus Christ, who has haunted human history, stood that day widening the gulf between His personal disciples and that great host of people who listened out of curiosity. These soon left off hearing Him because they realized that His sayings were extremely searching and difficult.

The Jewish patriots were watching Jesus closely, sizing Him up. The oppressed nation had been hoping for a king of their own for a long while. They wanted someone to deliver them from the tyranny of Rome. They looked at this "miracle worker," Jesus of Nazareth, and thought, "Maybe he's up to it! He's a popular preacher. Many think he's a prophet. He appeals to the common people. Perhaps we could use him!"

It wasn't the first or the last time that men have tried to use Jesus for their own purposes, rather than surrendering to Him. They wanted Him to be their deliverer from Rome rather than the redeemer of their lives. The Jews recognized their oppressive burden of taxation and servitude. They knew how little their take-home pay was. But they did not understand the burden of their sin and the fatal sickness that warped their lives. They wanted a political leader rather than a personal Lord. They were far more interested in the present than in the future.

So are we. How easily we get all involved with the busy, pressing, insistent present that doesn't leave us time to think or to wait on God! The click of a door, the ring of a telephone, the appointment on a calendar, the demands that business makes on us—there is scarcely a moment left.

We become involved with so many things that, like the Jewish leaders, we would easily come to the place where we would be trying to use Jesus to get us out of the scrapes in which we find ourselves in this present world.

Do we not look for a God with a Santa Claus face who hides in a cuckoo clock and comes out by invitation only? We don't want Him to disturb us in our everyday lives. We want to do our own thing, make our own decisions, run our own lives. We don't give God much of a chance with us.

Suffering is an unpleasant part of the human condition, but a large area for almost everyone. That is why we need Jesus. Otherwise, we would have to walk alone. The heart that never feels sorrow cannot so keenly feel joy.

To many people, "Blessed are they that mourn, for they shall be comforted" is pure philosophy. Especially to the young it is a question of theory—strictly academic. But one of these days it will become personal in the life of every individual.

A woman in another land had many troubles and was feeling very sorry for herself. The missionary in her village said, "Take an empty bowl and go to each house, asking the head of the house where there has been no sorrow to give you a kernal of rice." The suffering one made her way from door to door, from house to house. Finally, coming back to the missionary compound, she held out the empty bowl.

Paradox

There are times when we face life with an empty bowl, and Jesus fills it with a paradox: "Blessed are they that mourn."

We need to be challenged by such a startling statement because our concept of happiness is really very immature. Who would congratulate a man whose face is covered with scar tissue? Who would rejoice with a man because he failed? Our generation thinks of happiness and success as synonymous. We want to buy our books and our clothes and our commodities with a money-back guarantee if we are not satisfied. And we are shocked when we find that in reality we are refusing to be satisfied with life itself. You can't take it back, you have to live it out. If you don't know God, you have to make it by yourself.

We naturally think of sorrow as something to be shunned. Yet normal grief is not a disgrace. Rather, tears wash our eyes and water our hearts. Jesus actually calls mourning a benediction. What kind of puzzle is this?

Our modern-version beatitude seems to be, "Happy are the hard-boiled, for they never let life hurt them." In other words, happy is the guy who charges like a bulldozer and says, "I'm not going to let the world run over me!"

We greet each other, "Happy Birthday," and "Happy New Year," but we never seriously consider "Good Grief." It has become just a tag-phrase used by a cartoon character. When I saw it in print the first time, I turned away from it. I felt the expression violated every feeling of sympathy. It was shocking to me.

Ian Maclaren, the great Scottish preacher, said, "Remember, pastors, there are burdened hearts in every congregation." Many hearts share their burdens, but often heavier griefs are hidden. There are secret troubles and tears are shed where no eye but God sees them fall.

Does Jesus have a panacea for the unknown, for un-shared, unrevealed burdens? What is the purpose of saying, "Blessed are they that mourn"? He must have been talking about something we do not readily understand.

Purpose

Dr. B. H. Carroll used to say that in a Scripture passage there was often a "shell meaning" and a "kernel meaning." The latter implies its *purpose*.

In the original language, this word translated "mourn" is a very strong word for sadness. It means what it says—and worse. The English language possesses no single word sufficient to say, "Blessed is the individual who laments before God, who is saddened in heart and soul."

Some people are saddened only for the things of this world, for passing fame and fortune. Such sorrows are not uplifting, they have no redemptive quality. You can mourn in self-pity the rest of your life and become a worse individual, not a better one, because of it. There are sorrows that have redemptive qualities, that make us better people for having passed through the refiner's fire.

A person mourning is not to be confused with one who simply has a melancholy disposition, who is a deliberate pessimist, sad of countenance and belligerent of mind. Finding nothing good, sour toward everything in the world. This is not what Jesus was talking about. It's just a sinful disposition.

There is some mourning that we indulge in that is not profitable because it is selfish. Remember Ahab? He wanted Naboth's vineyard. It was a thing of convenience to him, a playthink, a nearby piece of real estate that would enhance his own extensive acreage. What it meant to Naboth to own it as a heritage from his fathers meant nothing to Ahab. Some don't care what things mean to other people. Deeply emotional feelings are trampled on by some without any concern at all. Ahab acted like a grown-up baby. He had become accustomed to getting his own way because he was king, and his power made him cruel.

"It is the heritage of my fathers," Naboth said. "I cannot sell it."

Ahab went to bed and cried all day. Now that helped everybody, including himself—weeping over something so insignificant! His wife, more evil than her childish husband, managed to have Naboth murdered so that her husband could have his toy.

King David mourned about the consequences of his sin. Many of his psalms are full of it, but he always ended by looking to God for forgiveness, strength, and help.

His predecessor, King Saul, whom Samuel rebuked publicly and declared that God would take the kingdom from him, mourned only over the realization that he was caught in front of his people. Here is one of the most revealing reflectors of a selfish personality, one of the brightest mirrors one could hold up before some tear-filled eyes.

King Saul looked in vain for friends among his countrymen. The nation had once admired him and looked up to him, but he had acted so small that, although he was a man "head and shoulders above the other men" he had become a little man in their eyes. These petulant words came from the disturbed king: "There is none of you that is sorry for me!" (1 Samuel 22:8). He mourned with self-pity.

There are some people who would not trade the luxury of self-pity for any blessing in the world. They wallow in it, they glory in it, they magnify it. It is the medication of their life.

It wasn't far from where King Saul reigned that later another man knelt to pray. We do not hear him indulging in self-pity. Wearing the sacred shoes of Scripture, with a searching soul and listening ears, we find Jesus praying in the Garden of Gethsemane, "Not *my* will, but Thine be done!"

All the sorrow and agony of all the ages of earth was dumped down on Jesus. His cup of suffering was running over with the bitter brine of our sins. The only thing we hear from the lips of Jesus was, "O my Father, if it be possible, let this cup pass from me; nevertheless, not as I will, but as thou wilt" (Matthew 26:39).

He was not feeling sorry for Himself. His mourning was for us—for the whole world of mankind. Such mourning is but another and deeper side of loving. Even on His way to death He said, "Daughters of Jerusalem, weep not for me, but weep for yourselves, and for your children" (Luke 23:28). He never told us to weep for His death, but to weep over the sin that caused His death.

"And there appeared an angel unto him from heaven, strengthening him" (Luke 22:43). The word "angel" means "a messenger"—what form he had I do not know. Many times, God would use us as angels to wipe the eyes and the brows and the hurts of our fellow men if we would let Him. But we are often like the disciples who remained at the outer gate, asleep—asleep to the great tragedies of life, asleep in the great crises of life, asleep through the great opportunities of life.

The greatest revolution the world has ever known, the Russian Revolution, has observed now more than fifty anniversaries. Do you know what the church was doing the day the revolution broke out? A great Church body was in session in Moscow, heatedly discussing whether the sashes on the priests' robes should be four inches off the floor or six! Things that mattered not—meeting no human need!

Was Jesus talking about mourning at funerals? Perhaps partly, but that is not the only meaning. At Palestinian funerals they hired mourners for pay. We usually bury above our ability, and so did those who lived in that poverty-stricken land. Secular history tells us that even the poorest funerals had "two paid flutes and a wailing woman"—the quotation was common in New Testament times. At a funeral, whoever made the loudest noise, whoever could muster the most flutes, was considered most grieved for his dead relative. This was no healing balm to a child weeping for its mother or a man weeping for his companion. Regardless of who a man paid to wail, he had to suffer his own loss.

Sometimes it seems that we also want paid mourners. We have "Dial-a-prayer," where someone else does our praying for us. Let the pastors, doctors, florists and morticians minister to the ill and bereaved in our place. But, regardless of what we do, a sorrowing heart has a need that is never met until that heart meets with God in a private relationship.

Cornelius, the Roman centurion of Acts 10, was a devout man, one who worshipped God. He mourned for a better relationship, for an understanding of God. His mourning was a sign of hope for what could still be. He sacrificed and prayed for it.

God laid His hand on Simon Peter and sent him to preach to the household of Cornelius.

Today we need similar divine discontent. We need people who are dissatisfied with sin, dissatisfied with life, dissatisfied with themselves, because "Blessed are they that mourn." We need to consider seriously our relationship to God and to our fellow men, and we rarely see the truths of God in joyful days. How long has it been since you mourned over sin? How long has it been since you had a burden for others? How long has it been since you walked alongside a friend and said, "Let me help you carry the load"? The true mourner is sensitive to the ills of the world.

A woman came to Jesus in great distress, wringing her hands. "Have mercy on me, O Lord, thou son of David," she cried, "my daughter is grievously vexed with a devil" (Matthew 15:22). How long has it been since we have come to God with mourning and asked help for our children and for ourselves? There must be purpose in our mourning!

Praise

As we *praise* God, our spirits are caught up in a vision of God's glory. We become like Isaiah—repentant, cleansed, empowered. God does not need our praise as much as we need to worship Him! The command is not for His sake, but for our own.

Sinclair Lewis, in his own egotism, did not recognize that when he said, "I'd have nothing to do with a God who demanded that I praise him all the while."

Luke quotes Jesus as saying, "Blessed are ye that weep now; for ye shall laugh" (Luke 6:21). Jesus Himself wept over one man, Lazarus. Then he wept over an entire city, Jerusalem. In Gethsemane, He agonized over the sins of the whole world. Isaiah foretold that He would be "a man of sorrows and acquainted with grief."

You may say, "I can't see anything good about sorrow!" There is nothing more pathetic than eyes that are dull, that are clouded with lack of recognition, that reflect no feeling. What God says to us is, "Blessed is that man who has not lost his capacity for concern." He still feels deeply about his brother's ills. He is still concerned about the cities of the world. There's not anything worse than a man who has lost his compassion. He always has dry eyes. When he gives his dollar, he feels like he has paid his dues to God and the human race.

Where there is no grief, there can be no comfort. Sorrow is not good in itself, and mourning is not blessed in itself. But blessed indeed is that man who finds consolation in his Lord. He enjoys a closeness of fellowship that he could never experience otherwise because of the presence of God. It is not in the mourning the blessing lies, but in the comfort of God.

Martin Luther re-phrased this beatitude: "Blessed are the sorrow-bearing—those who bear sorrow." And blessed is that man who mourns over himself, as did Paul, and says, "Oh, wretched man that I am! Who shall deliver me from the body of this death?" (Romans 7:24).

In a certain novel the story is written that a child was killed by a mad dog. The neighbors turned on the dog's owner, not realizing the guilt and sorrow the man already felt. He became a marked man, avoided and ostracized. This went on for a long while. Finally a drought came. The land was bare and seed scarce. The man who owned the dog sowed the last of his seed and the wind blew it out. The neighbors said, "It is a curse on him!"

But the father of the dead child went and sowed the other man's field in the night. When the neighbors found out what he had done they asked, "Why did you do that?" The grieved father answered, "Because I couldn't let God die in my heart."

If you do not mourn for others, if you have no concern for others, if you show no compassion for others, you will find that God seems dead and you live in a haunted house.

On a German castle, a man strung wires from tower to tower to make a giant wind harp. The job was finished in the summer and there was no music in the quiet nights. When the autumn winds came, there were some sounds, but during the violent storms of winter the full symphony rang out. Such a harp is the human heart. Real music is never present when you are just patting your feet. It comes in the storms, when you are searching your soul, and you find the sweet, answering voice of God ringing in your ears.

At the very end of the Bible we find the precious promise, "God will wipe away all tears from their eyes" (Revelation 21:4). He is the God of all comfort, therefore "Blessed are they that mourn, for they shall be comforted."

Blessed are the meek

Chapter 3

The Might of the Meek

The third in our set of stairs toward heavenly blessing on earth is the beatitude, "Blessed are the meek, for they shall inherit the earth" (Matthew 5:5).

Some believe that the beatitudes are paired—the first and second linked together, the third and fourth, the fifth and sixth, the seventh and eighth. Each of a pair supplements the other, and each pair builds on the preceding ones.

If Jesus had begun by saying, "Blessed are the meek," His listeners' hearts would scarcely have been prepared. He spoke first of being poor in spirit. It was only after a man recognized his poverty of spirit and need of forgiveness and comfort that he truly could see his own unworthiness. Then, with humility, he could approach the realization of genuine meekness and its reward.

In the Psalms we read, "But the meek shall inherit the earth, and shall delight themselves in the abundance of peace" (37:11). Also, "The meek will he guide in justice, and the meek will he teach his way" (25:9).

If we tried to name all the virtues, we might think of patience, courage, justice, and others. I doubt seriously if most people would mention meekness as a major virtue, a Christian adornment.

Words, like people, have a way of falling into poor company. Our definition of meekness today is far different from the implications of the word Jesus used. Its connotations and associations have changed.

This statement by Jesus was a paradox to those who listened to Him. The Jews were looking not only for a good life but a material kingdom. Much like people in our own day, they evidently felt that they wanted an affluent society, a stockpile of strength. Particularly, they were searching for a great leader who might free them from the domination of Rome. Many of these people hoped for a while that Jesus would become their earthly deliverer and ruler. Imagine their bitter disappointment when Jesus said, "Blessed are the meek, for they shall inherit the earth." These people wanted the earth right then and there. But they couldn't possibly imagine meekness inheriting anything.

Go to a military strategist planning world peace. Assert that the way to peace and tranquility is meekness. Indeed, you might find yourself on the front line of battle to see if you could find any meekness there. For this is not the concept of the world at all. Jesus was saying, "My kingdom is not like that. It is not what you think you want. It is not of this world." He did not teach advance by aggressiveness. He did not use the resources of force. He set forth meekness in contrast to the usual concepts of men.

What is meekness? We will take, first, the negative side. Usually we admire a driving personality. We think highly of ambition and success. We would not consider it a compliment if someone said about us, "He is meek as a lamb." Inside, we would withdraw from that. We get the connotation of a Mr. Milquetoast who stretches out his neck and says, "Please step on me . . . I needed that!"

Although we may not wish to be considered meek as a lamb, we know that the arch-enemy of the lamb has always been the wolf. And wolves have lost the battle—there are more sheep today in the world than wolves. It might do us good to realize that in the animal world those who have the greatest strength, the predators, are destroying themselves and being destroyed. The meekest ones, the gentle ones, are surviving.

What is meekness? We may look at one who is of a calm temperament and say, "How meek he is. How quiet he is." We may think lack of quarrelsomeness a Christian virtue and it may not be at all. It may be only a natural tendency, not a matter of facing up to ourselves. But Jesus said meekness is a Christian virtue. One sign of a Christian is meekness developed as the Spirit of God leads.

In Numbers 12:3 it is said, "Now the man Moses was very meek, above all the men who were upon the face of the earth." Aaron, the brother of Moses, did not possess the God-trained meekness of that great leader.

When the Israelites came to the foot of Mount Sinai, Aaron was left with responsibility for the people while Moses went up the mountain. He failed to measure up. "And when the people saw that Moses delayed to come down out of the mount, the people gathered themselves together unto Aaron, and said unto him, Up, Make us gods which shall go before us; for as for this Moses, . . . we know not what is become of him" (Exodus 32:1). Aaron took their gold earrings and made an idol in the shape of a calf, as the people wanted. That wasn't meekness, that was weakness! The Christian needs to understand the difference between the two. The Christian who does not speak of concerning his convictions is not meek at all, but weak and afraid, unwilling to face the real issues and the consequences of taking a stand.

Neither is meekness the same as slothfulness. Jesus was not talking about an individual who is too lazy to brush away the flies. Not using his talents, but claiming as an excuse that "the meek shall inherit the earth." Jesus had stern words for the man who would not use what had been entrusted to him. He described the punishment of the man who was given one talent and buried it: "Thou wicked and slothful servant, . . . Take, therefore, the talent from him, . . . And cast the unprofitable servant into outer darkness" (Matthew 25:26,28,30). Such a man was a burden to society, he didn't carry his own weight. He buried the light that God gave when it should have been set on a hill.

Meekness is not compromising for "peace at any price." Or saying, "I'd just rather get along without disagreements." There will always be enmity between God and this world. In reality meekness is compatible with great strength, great power, great composure—if you have those qualities you can walk softly and never have to use force.

Tamed

The Greek word, in the language of the Master's day, perhaps can best be translated "being *tamed*"—strength under control. In our dictionary today we find meekness defined as gentleness—and it is that. In the American Southwest we immediately think of breaking wild horses or of training young horses to harness or bridle.

But if you look further in the dictionary, you will find meekness also defined as "self-surrender." That characterizes the individual who has won the battle with himself, with his fellow men and with his God. "I do not own myself," he is saying, "and I will allow no man to own me; I am not for sale, but I surrender myself to a higher cause"—that is being tamed.

This word was common in the language of the Master's day and usually pictured a giant animal, straining every muscle, having great power. But only after the horse was broken, tamed, was he of any value for work. Concerning the Christian, Jesus said that only when we are broken, only when we are tamed, only when we are willing to surrender ourselves to Him, can we inherit His earth—that is genuine meekness.

The comparable Hebrew word perhaps gives us a better understanding. It actually says, "being molded." Meekness is not something you buy over the counter. It is a virtue you cannot develop in a day. Rather, it is something that must be worked at constantly. Sometimes the lips may have to be sealed, words have to be kept back, and knuckles become white, but nothing is said. Meekness is character being molded in the fire.

A young child is not left alone to roam freely in a room with an open fire, because he might be burned. When he is placed in the playpen, he is being molded to discipline, yet as far as he is concerned, those pieces of wood are just as much of a jail as iron bars. He has to be trained with certain restraints; he has to face up to certain limitations; he has to be hemmed in until he is mature enough to protect himself.

A further example of meekness, of being tamed, of being molded, was Paul, the great apostle. In his early days, he persecuted the Church vigorously. An arrogant Jew, he was traveling to Damascus from Jerusalem, planning to punish many Christians as heretics and criminals, which he considered them to be. He was anxious to crush this false religion, as he considered it.

Saul of Tarsus was a brilliant and well-educated young man, but he had not come under the discipline of God. He had to learn the truth of the proverb, "He that is slow to anger is better than the mighty; and he that ruleth his spirit, than he that taketh a city" (Proverbs 16:32).

We find God taming this man on the road to Damascus. God blinded him first so that he could not see, then gave him inner sight so he would look up toward heaven and see the Son of God, whom he would not look at before. We hear him say, "Lord, what wilt thou have me to do?"

This mighty man who delighted in destroying Christ's church was reborn. He was transformed until he became a channel for the power of God greater than anyone else in the New Testament. Saul became Paul. He was made over, he was made meek and teachable. We also can be changed.

Paul told Timothy to "stir up the gift of God, which is in thee," and urged Timothy to "follow after righteousness, godliness, faith, love, patience, meekness" (1 Timothy 6:11). "For God hath not given us the spirit of fear, but of power, and of love, and of a sound mind" (2 Timothy 1:6,7). This was how the young man would gain strength to stand in the storms that would break over him.

Teachable

Another definition of meekness is, "Blessed is that man who is *teachable*." Some you cannot teach anything. Their hearts were closed long ago, their minds made up. They think they know all the answers, yet they are not accomplishing anything, they are not discovering anything, they are not curing any of the world's ills. Only one who can learn can become meek. Meekness is indeed a teachable condition.

Will Rogers was perhaps one of the most famous and best-loved figures in recent United States history. Why? Could it be because he said, "I never met a man I couldn't like"? It was a very wise man who was really saying, "I never met a man who couldn't teach me something."

Lloyd C. Douglas was once a mediocre writer who had not achieved any great success. One day he was in a store and a clerk, recognizing him, said, "Mr. Douglas, you have the ability to use words, you can put things down in writing. Sir, have you ever wondered what happened to that seamless robe they gambled for at the foot of the cross?" And Lloyd Douglas, a man with a teachable mind, went back to his study and turned loose his imagination on that idea, the inspiration from a clerk who had given his mind a challenge that he had never faced before. After much thought and work, he gave the world one of the best-known religious novels of our century.

The Pharisees were not teachable. One prayed, "Lord, I thank thee that I am not as other men are." They had fixed ideas. When Jesus cut across their ideas, they plotted to put Him to death.

Where you work, people are not interested in anyone who has that Pharisee's attitude in life. Nobody is going to be interested in your witness. But they will be very interested in one who is interested in them—but their life, their children, their family, their hopes, their aspirations.

You have to talk about them, to ask about them. This meekness many faithful church-goers have long forgotten.

Modern transportation and communication have made the world a neighborhood. But we have not yet made it a brotherhood. That cannot come to pass until Christians adopt a concept of compassion which is synonymous with meekness of attitude. We must recognize that meekness is the highest type of courage.

Daniel displayed courage with an attitude of meekness. The ruler of his conquered nation decreed that no man should pray to any god, only to the dictator. "Now when Daniel knew that the writing was signed, he went into his house; and his windows being open in his chamber toward Jerusalem, he kneeled upon his knees three times a day, and prayed, and gave thanks before his God, as he did aforetime" (Daniel 6:10).

If such a decree should be made in our city and the churches should be closed, what would be our reaction? We may yet desperately need such courage as Daniel's in our time. A long while before Simon Peter, Daniel recognized that "We ought to obey God rather than men" (Acts 5:29).

The difference is that in our society today we worry about whether God is alive or not. In Old Testament days they just thought about God keeping them alive. That's a strange shift in values, isn't it? Daniel believed that God was alive and therefore with great courage he went on to face life—or death in the lions' den.

Centuries before, God said to Joshua, "See, I have given

into thine hand Jericho, and its king, and the mighty men of valor" (Joshua 6:2). Joshua was afraid, but with courage he surrounded Jericho and God kept His word.

The great lawgiver, Moses, was the only Bible character compared to Jesus in this matter of meekness. But Moses was not always that disciplined. There had been a time when murder came into his heart, when anger was him greatest problem. The welfare of his fellow man wasn't always his first thought, but rather self-preservation. God began to tame Moses—his spirit, his disposition, his attitude. At last he put himself into the will of God and God began to mold him. Moses became mighty under God's command to lead his people from the place of bondage into a place of service.

Meekness, for a child of God, means self-control.

Napoleon, the conqueror of many nations, said concerning Jesus: "Alexander, Charlemagne, and I have conquered men by force, but Jesus of Nazareth conquered by love."

Hitler conquered Paris in World War II, and the crumbling city acquiesed to his demands. He stood under the Eiffel Tower and said, "I have conquered you by force, but now I shall win you by love." But you can never win by love that which you have forced. Hitler never really won Paris, for the city realized that he did not understand love.

In a parable, Jesus gave His disciples the implied command, "Go out into the highways and hedges, and compel them to come in" (Luke 14:23). In the first century, a general decided to make Christians out of his army. He led his legions up to a river and said, "Now go down into the water!" and they were baptized as a regiment. But they did not become Christians by riding their horses into a river at the command of their general.

Tempered

Compulsory religion cannot change the inner life of a man. True discipleship characterizes only a life that has been reborn, refined as gold, and *tempered* as steel. Even Jesus Himself was tempered and forged in the battle of temptation.

In the Old Testament, Joseph knew what poise, character, and self-control were before he became viceroy of Egypt.

Esau lacked courage to be willing to minister as God required of the firstborn. His brother Jacob left home, casting his fate upon the Lord, and God made him into Israel, godly founder of a nation.

Peter lacked self-control until the power of the Holy Spirit of God made him a different man at Pentecost.

Keeping your mouth shut, being cowardly, just saying, "I'll walk out, I'll have nothing to do with it" is not meekness! Meekness is a fruit of the Spirit, but the fruit of the Spirit is meekness—not weakness.

The first beatitude says that the poor in spirit shall inherit the kingdom of God, the third says the meek shall inherit the earth. Does that interest you? Are you concerned about inheriting the earth?

This beatitude came from the lips of Jesus as He knew it from Psalm 37:11, "But the meek shall inherit the earth." Yet Jesus also spoke of His kingdom being not of this world, but a spiritual kingdom. The Christian who lives in meekness does not have to wait until he dies to experience some of the kingdom that God has promised right here on earth, knowing the peace and joy of God's presence with us.

How much of the earth do you possess? And how much of the earth possesses you? Do you possess your possessions or do your possessions possess you? Although we have inherited this earth, we sometimes allow it to possess us.

One of our young men going away into military service spoke to me in the aisle one Sunday. "I shall have to take leave from our church for a while," he said. But I felt that lad would never take leave from a church wherever he found himself.

A pastor, when a young man sat in his office just before going away into the service asked, "Are you afraid of what you are going to?" The young man answered with a great deal of discernment. "Pastor," he said, "I'm not afraid of what I'm going to as much as what I may come back to." What are we leaving? What do we have to give wherever we go?

The man who inherits the earth is the man who finds a tranquility within himself. He lives peaceably. You inherit a lot of earth when you conquer the territory of your own soul! You have conquered worlds when you have lived amicably with your fellow men. For the man who has a confidence in himself, yet lives in meekness toward his fellow man, is really the only one who is at home in this world. He is able to possess it by God's grace.

When you sit in the evening and watch the sun go down and the stars come out, do you have tranquility of spirit because this beauty is yours?

Christ said, "I am yours, and in Me you possess everything—ye shall inherit the earth!" That was His spirit: meekness, not arrogance. Submitting to Him in meekness, you will find that you grow into those virtues which are most precious in His sight.

He is God; I am His; the world is mine!

Blessed are they which do hunger and thirst

Chapter 4

The Quest for Quality

To the crowd assembled on the mountain later known as "The Mount of Beatitudes," Jesus said, "Blessed are they which do hunger and thirst after righteousness, for they shall be filled" (Matthew 5:6). A little later, He pointed out the direction our search should take: "But seek ye first the kingdom of God, and his righteousness, and all these things shall be added unto you" (Matthew 6:33).

Is this beatitude relevant for us today, in our age? Our physical hunger for food is easily filled, because there are snack bars on almost every corner, perhaps all night restaurants in any town. At picnics now, women seem to trade diets instead of recipes.

What picture comes to mind when we think of hunger and thirst? Poverty may not be relevant to your own life, but it is a present reality in our world. There may be as many people living in poverty in our time as in the last United States depression, and likely there is more poverty in most parts of the world because of the population explosion of recent years. Poverty is on every hand.

This is a strange and strong beatitude Jesus spoke, yet immediately He was within the hearts and minds of these people. His words were relevant to them when He said, "Blessed are those who hunger and thirst." Many of them had made journeys across the trackless deserts and wastelands, hunting one oasis after another, and finding more mirages in their minds than oases in their lives.

Without any weather reports, without any warning, they would be beset by gusting wind and stinging sand, and the moving dunes would wipe out all human tracks. As they tried to turn their bodies away from blinding sand, its thickness would hinder breathing and settle on their hair, hands, face, clothes. Then came thirst, almost unquenchable. They would wonder if they might never see their homes again.

The people of Jesus' time were not unmindful of what it meant to hunger, for they had no refrigeration or supermarkets. When company came at night, as was the custom because of heat, if a family did not have sufficient bread left from that day, they would have to go to the next house to beg or borrow. Jesus used this custom as basis for a parable. There was no deep freeze, no open-all-night stand, and in many cases no credit. It was not unusual for a mother to watch her child die of malnutrition. Jesus was speaking to a half-starved world. Then how could He say to these people, "Happy, happy are those who hunger and thirst"?

Have you ever been hungry? A young man went out to serve with a certain group, and he felt he was not adjusting or communicating. One evening he admitted it aloud, and one of the fellows spoke up, saying, "Have you ever been hungry? That's what makes us tick!"

Then Jesus came to an important definitive word when He said, "thirst after *righteousness.*" And He offered a promise of immediate reward: "they shall be filled!"

Do we have any conception at all of what Jesus meant when he used the word "righteousness"? Ours is an age of relative morality—many call it a "new morality," as though it had no relation to the Scriptures at all or to the moral principles of past days. Righteousness—God's righteousness—is a fixed and unalterable standard.

Jesus was asking, "Have you ever been hungry spiritually?" Have you ever been hungry to the extent that you really were glad that somebody said, "It's Sunday, and we are going to church"? Do you ever feel with the psalmist, "I was glad when they said unto me, Let us go into the house of the Lord" (Psalm 122:1)? Or is that verse just something for the children to memorize, recite, and forget just as soon as they are able to buy a car or a boat of their own?

Have you ever been hungry? What are your hungers? You probably have some want, some desire—some prayer of yours has gone unanswered. Some of our desires will end in loss and frustration, of course, with unsatisfactory answers. Nevertheless, we wait upon the Lord in faith, knowing that He will fully reward His children.

Philosophers of all ages have wearied themselves in vain trying to define the ideal life. What is man's chief good?

William Blake, genius of a past century, put on canvas the picture of a little man standing at the foot of a ladder reaching to the moon. The title of the picture put words into the mouth of the man as he reached up: "I Want!" Man is wanting incarnate. The question is not, Do you want? It is simply a matter of *what* you want! It determines your destiny.

Now that man has been to the moon, that particular desire is to some extent satisfied. But maybe that's part of our problem. Although men have been through the heavens, that doesn't mean we have seen the eternal God of the heavens. And has it made the world a happier place to live? If we ceased trying to out-brag the rest of the world, if the noise of the circus died out, would we feel like crying out, "Stop the world, I want to get off!"?

If we become quiet, and in the stillness recognize the sovereignty of God, would we be willing to walk with Him as God? Or would the very thought that He is still around frighten us? Where is our quest for quality? What is our standard of values? Inflation and deflation make prices fluctuate, but what has happened to our individual sense of values? Have they gone up and down as much as the rest of the world's?

Outside a little village called Warren, Ohio, is a spot that is supposed to be the geographic center of the world.

The sign there reads: "This is the center of the world . . . you can go anywhere from here."

In His Sermon on the Mount, Jesus was marking out the center of God's standards of value. He was talking to people about their basic wants and needs and appetites. Let us not think for a moment that all the evil appetites of the world exist in other places. Not all the users of dope are in New York City; not all the illegitimacy is in Chicago; not all the hippies are in San Francisco; not all the sin is in the neighboring cities! Wherever basic appetites exist, wherever there is hunger, wherever there is man, what he does with his desires determines his destiny. Man becomes what he wants: "he shall be filled."

Random Hungers

But many of the things we want are merely *random hungers*. Some of them are haunting! You bury them and they won't stay buried, not even for three days. They have a resurrection every time they come to mind. We have second-rate or low-grade hungers, chasing after frivolous things that do not matter in the scale and scope of eternity.

Vance Packard wrote a book called *The Status Seekers*, in which he showed how cleverly the American people have been made captive to the "hidden persuaders" of our culture. Secular society revolves around desire for momentary things—not values that last, but ephemeral or material things. We are much like children with a little bit of money, rushing into a dime store a few days before Christmas, "not seeking anything but wanting everything."

Often we have no clear definition of goal or real purpose in life. We wind up much like the day after Christmas, floors strewn with gift-wrappings of the things we never really wanted. Toys we played with a while, broke them, and were through with them.

A boy I once knew had a momentary desire to chase a large butterfly and he pursued the beautiful, fluttering creature a long way. Hours later, made aware he was missing, half the little town in which we lived was hunting the boy. On horseback, by foot, up and down the creek bed and along the river they looked and called. Finally he was found safe, but the butterfly had eluded him.

Alexander the Great, with an unhealthy lust for power, conquered and crushed the world of his day. Then he sat down and wept like a schoolboy because that world didn't satisfy him; there was nothing left to grab, nothing more the whet his desire for power, nothing out there to satisfy his taste for bloodshed.

Greedy King Midas, when promised anything he wanted, asked that everything he touched should be turned into gold. Soon he was begging for that remarkable power to be removed. It immobilized his daughter and ruined his food.

In the questing search of man, there is an ego problem. John Ruskin called it the search for applause. This is one of the random hungers, the hunger for an "image" that satisfies our pride.

There have been selfish, random, haunting hungers in every man. Many make themselves a little "god" to their own dimensions, to fit their own desires. Your children probably sense that what you do with yourself on Sunday morning is pretty much the fulfillment of the real desires of your life.

Some people have created "gods" to pray to during fearful hours in hospital corridors—but left them there. Some concepts of God have been shaped in a foxhole—and left there. Some people have crawled out from under a weight of tragedy vowing, "I will walk the straight and narrow from now on"—but they didn't. The experience haunted them for a little while, then they left it behind.

Reckless Hungers

Desires for deliverance, health, and happiness are legitimate hungers, but many desires evident in our society today are *reckless hungers*.

A reckless and irresponsible hunger today is manifested in drug abuse. Misguided experimenters say, "LSD is a lovely way to die!" They call it "a trip," when the mind leaves the body—I could not say enough against it! But we live in a society where the body often leaves the mind behind in a search for ego satisfaction, in lust for pleasure, in greed for thrills.

Our reckless hungers can be very harmful, very dangerous. So many times, the immediate pleasure and false fulfillment seem so alluring we do not recognize the long-term effects will be detrimental to our bodies and character. Many times, afterward, we utter the sad words, "If only I had it to do over, I would avoid that."

A child who was under the care of a nursemaid was giving a lot of trouble. He was crying and fretting because he could not have his way. His mother, in another room of the house, tired of the fuss, yelled out, "Just give him what he wants so he will be quiet!"

Moments later, she was startled by a scream of pain from her son. Rushing to see what was the matter, she found that the child had seen a beautifully colored insect and reached for it. It was a wasp, and the mother's helper, recognizing the danger and trying to avoid the child's hurt, had restrained him. But the mother's command was obeyed. This young child's reckless desire brought him pain and a hard-earned lesson. It happens that way with many of us.

When the prodigal son became hungry, he ate the husks that he fed the swine, but when he came near starvation, he thought of his father. He recognized there was nowhere else to go but back home. Other things did not satisfy; the excesses which led him to the hogpen only haunted him. In his heart was a hidden hunger.

A few years ago, the government made a film called "Hidden Hunger." It showed that in this affluent society of ours, where most people have more than enough to eat, where many are eating too much, people still suffer from physical malnutrition because they do not eat the right kinds of foods. The message of the film was that the physical body has hidden hungers for the things necessary for proper nutrition and good health.

Just as there were hidden hungers in the prodigal—the reckless hunger of his dissipation, the real hunger of his body, and the hidden hunger of his need for his family—there are also in every man. The quest often is ignored, sometimes forgotten, other times overlooked, but there is in every man a hidden spiritual hunger.

Redemptive Hungers

All other quests are fruitless unless we find God. Our deepest hunger will never be filled until we recognize that many of our hidden hungers are desires for God and for His righteousness. There are *redemptive hungers.*

What is righteousness? There are several things meant by hungering and thirsting after righteousness. It is a matter of being right, of being justified, of having a right relationship with God. Who is righteous? Only God. In other words, Jesus said, "Blessed is that man who hungers after God."

Do you have any hunger for God today? Or do you come into a church service without desire for God? Do you fail to worship? Do you leave as empty-hearted as you came? If you don't get much out of church, what kind of appetite did you bring with you? Have you lost your first love, and thus your appetite for God?

When the Moslems enter their mosques, they leave their shoes outside the door. Often we seem to come into our churches and leave our heads and hearts outside. Some men perhaps feel they would trade worship for any excuse if they could just get the service over. They have no real hunger, no spiritual capacity.

You may say it is up to the preacher to create an appetite. But the psalmist exhorted, "Oh, taste and see that the Lord is good!" (Psalm 34:8). Some have never had their appetite whetted, their taste tested. They have never experienced the blessing of an encounter with God. Rather, they think of a Santa Claus relationship: "Give me . . . give me!" This is a cheap dimension of divine relationship, not the highest and best. With God, righteousness is quite synonymous with our salvation, in its most complete sense.

Charles Spurgeon had the privilege of preaching to more than six thousand people each Sunday. One day he received an anonymous letter. "Unless you give me a large amount of money, I shall say certain things about you," it threatened. Spurgeon wrote back, publishing it publicly, "You and the likes of you may say all you wish about me!" He was a man at peace with himself, his fellow men, and his God. He had tasted of the "peace that passeth understanding."

Isaiah cried out to his people, "Wherefore do you spend money for that which is not bread? And your labor for that which satisfieth not?" (Isaiah 55:2–3). Why do we not hunger for the eternal God?

Two 18-year-olds recently were sentenced by a judge to eat baby food. "You have acted like children," he said, "so you will eat like children." For a given number of days they had to eat strained carrots and spinach and custards —spoon-fed like babies. The apostle Paul told the Corinthians that he was still having to feed them milk when they ought to be eating meat. They were babies; they were carnal; they had not grown up. We also fail, so often, to develop maturity in our ideas of God and strength in spiritual things.

God does not practice "forced feedings." But the Good Shepherd offers green pastures and the Holy Spirit creates in us, initially and continually, a redemptive hunger for the holy.

In your highest moments, when you are your best self, what do you really want out of life? What is that highest purpose of your existence? What do you want to do?

Mankind has the impulse toward happiness, and he who searches has at least the reward of not being content unless he grows and develops. And he has a responsibility to others. One of our well-known gospel songs begins, "I would be true, for there are those who trust me."

Paul had a way of singling out this highest hunger, the redemptive hunger, the hunger for God. He declared that he stripped himself down to essentials so that he would not be burdened with material things and selfish desires. He refused to be perturbed about his surroundings; he had learned to accept whatsoever state he found himself in. He had learned to live not for himself but in Christ. Outside things could not bother him. With singlemindedness he vowed, "This one thing I do: I strive to be like Christ!"

75

Each of us have to make up our minds, because we are going to become what we think and do. What is life's chief, highest, noblest purpose? And when will the moment come that our greatest desire is fulfilled?

I trust it will be, as it should, that time when we meet Christ face to face and hear His "Well done, thou good and faithful servant!"

Blessed are the merciful

Chapter 5

The Mystery of Mercy

Quoting the Beatitudes is easy. Most children who attend Bible School memorize them. Along with the 23rd Psalm and John 3:16, the Beatitudes are early assignments.

In conversation, we may have used them over and over until they have ceased to mean much. Ours is a hardened age and these strange, deeply meaningful words seem not to penetrate our souls. And if we speak such a message without love, it cannot be effective.

In the fifth beatitude, the Master was talking about forgiveness: "Blessed are the merciful," He said, "for they shall obtain mercy" (Matthew 5:7).

This seems the simplest of the beatitudes, but in reality it is the most searching. Anyone would probably agree, "Sure, this is a decent thing. It's just another way of stating the Golden Rule. If you do good to others they will naturally come around and do good to you."

Not always! You do good to some people and you cause them to wonder. Even if they don't say it aloud, they think, "What's got into that guy? What's his angle?" Sometimes we find that befriending people, forgiving them, having the spirit of Christ toward them, will elicit a suspicious attitude. They misjudge our motives and question our good sense and see how much they can impose on us.

The fifth beatitude sounds like the theme of a movie script where everything always comes out all right. Someone does something kind for another who, years later, comes back and does something kind in return. Good is always compensated, and right will triumph, and it's just the thing people like to see.

George Bernard Shaw portrayed this in one of his most famous plays, *Adronacles and the Lion*. His character walked through the jungle and met a lion in great pain with an infected thorn in its paw. Because of its distress, the lion was too weak to be dangerous. The man took out the thorn, poured alcohol into the wound and went his way. Years later the man, a Christian, was thrown into an arena to be torn by wild beasts. This lion recognized him, nestled up against him and protected him from the others, letting the man know it remembered his kind deed in removing the thorn from its paw. Such a pat reward is effective on the stage and in movie scripts, but good deeds do not always work out that way on the real stage called life.

Be prepared for the fact that even those to whom you are most merciful may turn around and misuse you at the first opportunity. It is not what they do to you or do not do to you—your attitude is what Jesus is speaking about. He was saying, "I want you to have the enduring power of the Spirit of God that you survive. For your soul's sake, I want you to have the loving compassion of God, the unselfish desires of God."

Jesus, in His Sermon on the Mount, moved from one great statement of reality to another. Perhaps here he found the first negative reaction, when he told them to be merciful to all people. He was speaking to an audience that didn't want mercy for other people, especially their oppressors. They had been reared on the "eye for an eye and tooth for a tooth"—blood for blood, insult for insult, feud for feud.

This nation had been harassed, taxed, burned, whipped, stoned. Jesus was talking to men who nursed revolution in their breasts, dreaming and planning vengeance, hoping for a great deliverer in their time to break the bondage of Rome. They were looking for a leader; in fact, they were looking Jesus over, wondering if He could be the right one. He had eloquence. He was able to do great miracles, and this always attracted crowds of people. The leaders of the Jews were sizing Him up to see if this man could wear an earthly crown as leader of their cause.

But Jesus' words did not sound like those of a military dictator: "Be merciful to people and you will obtain mercy." Notice He didn't say, "You will obtain mercy from other people," but just "You shall obtain mercy." All graveside, foxhole, or hospital-corridor promises are not kept. Mercies are not paid back like a debt in the same coin.

Jesus' audience began to recognize that He was not speaking just beautiful phrases. Somehow He was able to look past their masks and penetrate their hearts. Just as His words speak to yours and mine now.

We have to realize that judgment of evildoers is the only thing that God doesn't need our help with. "Vengeance is mine; I will repay, saith the Lord" (Romans 12:19). He asks us to help in the singing. He asks us to help in the preaching. He asks us to help in the praying. He asks us to help with witnessing and visitation, but He declared, "Vengeance is *mine! I* will repay."

Hate can never have the last word—not in a nation, not in a church, not in a man. Will we never learn that in trying to destroy others we first destroy ourselves? Moving up on somebody to get even, or, as the young people say, "to get the edge on" somebody, brings its own disaster.

You will find yourself, trying to get the edge on somebody, going over the edge. Down, down, down goes that individual whose mind and heart, whose thoughts and attitude are given over to hatred, bitterness, and getting even. Hate is contagious. It passes from one generation to another, teaching a child to hate before he learns what it is to love and shaping him to ruin all the lives he touches.

Once I held a funeral where one half of the family sat

on one side and the other half on the other. Neither group spoke to the other. They even went out at different times. I asked one of the grandchildren, "Why is your grandfather mad at your great-uncle that they would not speak to each other at your great-grandmother's funeral?"

"I really don't know," he answered. "I don't remember what it was, but it must have been something bad, because we have been divided over it all our lives."

Dr. W. A. Criswell tells of a church that split over where they should locate the piano. Some wanted it on the left side of the pulpit and some on the right side. Twenty five years later the leader of the movement that split the church couldn't remember which side he had voted on himself.

"I will repay, saith the Lord." Charles Haddon Spurgeon spoke a great truth, a Biblical truth, when he said, "God will measure us with our own check-lists." No other beatitude makes it so plain that we *are* the result, we *make* the result, and we *become* that result!

More Than Tears

To be merciful is a solemn admonition of the Lord, and to be merciful is *more than tears*, it is merciful action. It is more than just kind deeds, for to do kind things without kind thoughts involves us in hypocrisy. If we do it only professionally, as a social-acting and thinking person, and not individually, if we do it because we see a need and not because our best self rises to that need, we are seeking only self-glory.

Some very merciless people can weep abundant tears when they feel it is appropriate for the occasion. The merciful also weep, but they do it without staging and without props; they weep because their hearts weep. The difference lies in the attitude of the person. Those who are influenced only by the emotional circumstances that surround them and not by the love of God prompting their hearts are not truly merciful.

Precious indeed are the words in the eleventh chapter of John, "Jesus wept." This merciful Savoir wept over the loss of a friend, even though He knew that Lazarus would live again on earth. Why did He weep, knowing that death held no dominion over His friend? Why do we weep when we know that death holds no dominion over our loved ones? We weep because it is human to weep. We weep over the psychological amputation, we weep for the loneliness of separation, we weep because of our loss. No man is an island, and we weep because we are part of one another.

Jesus did weep, not counting the sorrow of His friends as nothing. He did not weep for Lazarus, He wept for that emptiness He felt when He came for the first time to this familiar house and Lazarus was not there. The Master sensed our feeling of a house when it is empty—the rooms are there, the furniture is there, but without the loved one, it holds a strange silence that often screams. Jesus saw what it did to Mary and Martha and, the Bible says, Jesus wept.

In the Old Testament, Jeremiah was called "the weeping prophet." He shed many tears over Israel because of her coming destruction.

Bear in mind that being merciful is more than just giving away hot coffee and warm doughnuts in times of natural disaster. The truly merciful are more than "professional do-gooders." Showing mercy is more than signing a donation card because you know if you don't you are going to be looked down on in your company—the boss expects to put a placard in the front window that says, "We are 100% signed up for the Community Chest."

On some things, you don't have much choice. There was never a time when people have given so much to charitable things and so little of themselves in a charitable spirit. These has never been a time, I say, when we have given so much for charitable institutions and given so little of ourselves in service. We feel that as long as we have given money, we are free from other responsibility—but appointed supervisor of everything! A donation is just the first step of mercy.

Mercy is far more than that. The dictionary defines it as being full of pity and compassion, as opposed to censorious criticism.

In the story Jesus told, when a poor traveler was mugged on the road to Jericho, much to the eternal shame of the religious world, the priest and the Levite passed by on the other side. Some of us are about that far removed from the needs we encounter today; we send somebody else in our place.

"Let's pass a resolution," we say, or, "The government

ought to do something about it." But ministering to the needs of others ourselves, getting our hands dirty, maybe getting blood on our clothes, is unthinkable. The very idea of taking something out of our pockets makes us react angrily—but we give to the civic drives for many good secular causes.

"Why doesn't the church do something?" many ask. God created us as individuals and gave each of us individual responsibility. When a man joins the church and becomes part of the family of God, his relationship to the needs of society is not taken away. On an individual, personal basis, he is commanded to be merciful.

> Rise up, O men of God!
> Have done with lesser things:
> Give heart and mind and soul and strength
> To serve the King of kings.
>
> —William P. Merrill

Quit feeling that when you put something in the plate you have done about the biggest thing you can think of—tipping God! Ask how much of yourself—your heart, your concern, your prayers—have you put into a service? We pray for safe driving as we come to church, but do we pray that something will happen to us while we are there?

Inner Attitude

To be merciful reflects the inner life—the disposition of the soul, if you please. An *inner attitude* is what Jesus was talking about. When a person is merciful, the disposition of his soul is compassion, concern, empathy. Indifference is impossible. A man who has the attitude of God in him cannot ignore pain, poverty, injustice.

Mercy is a virtue of the Christian faith. It is not a luxury you pick up on the communion table for a given amount of dollars pledged to the church. It is more than good manners, good citizenship, or "being nice." Not only is it a virtue—hear me well!—it is going to be a necessity to everybody who lives here if this land of ours is to survive.

There was a time when we felt that all we had to do to keep our children from alcoholism was to vote liquor out of our precinct. But now we live in a very small world. Somebody from another precinct over the hill, or from the other side of the world, could meet our children in school and marry into our family. They could become a part of that which is dearest to us and yet have neither heard of our standards nor have our foundations. The more important thing is training the family that you send out into the world.

God declared that the wicked, the scorner, the rabble rouser will be shown no mercy. "For he shall have judgment without mercy, that hath shown no mercy" (James 2:13). God's judgment is a very stern thing. We have to recognize that God alone is able to assess and execute judgment. Sometimes to let a man have his own way is the most severe judgment you can mete out.

In one parable of Jesus, a man went to collect from another who owed him. He refused to have mercy

on the man who was in debt to him. Then his own creditor
came to collect, a man to whom he owed ten times more
than was owed him, and he pleaded for mercy. Like that
man, you and I are not only creditors, we are also debtors.
Certainly we cannot say that we have no need of the
mercies of God.

Stephen was an example of God's way of mercy. He
showed Christlikeness of spirit when he said of those who
stoned him, "Lord, lay not this sin to their charge" (Acts
7:60). Where did he learn it? From the Savior. And we
must learn it from the same great source—the Lord
Himself.

On the day of Christ's crucifixion, Simon of Cyrene
had no intention of carrying the cross of Jesus, for crosses
were to be avoided. Simon was from Africa and evidently
came to Jerusalem for the great passover ceremoney. The
moment the cross was thrust upon Simon, his trip to Jerusalem was ruined. He could not go into the temple, because he was ceremonially unclean. Though he lost his date
with the Temple of God in Jerusalem, he gained historical immortality through God's Son.

Though Simon failed to achieve his own plan, he became part of God's plan as he carried the cross for Jesus.
And he must have asked himself why Jesus was carrying
this cross. Later, his family is referred to as being in the
faith. He was called of God to the great task and his
merciful heart made the most out of it. Works and
faith can make a whole family Christian.

Likeness of God

To be merciful is to be in the *likeness of God*. Jesus said, "Be ye, therefore, merciful, as your Father also is merciful" (Luke 6:36). Do we have God's merciful attributes? It has been said of the early church that they were a group of ordinary men who learned the quality of mercy of their God.

"Merciful" in the Hebrew is a word that cannot be easily translated. It does not mean just that we feel sorry for someone, that we feel compassion or empathy. If it could be translated in idea, it would mean that somehow we get under another's skin, that we see through his eyes and feel with his heart. That's what being merciful means.

The American Indians have a prayer, "Great Spirit, grant that I may not criticize my neighbor until I have walked a mile in his moccasins." A wise sage put it, "To know all is to forgive all." This should not be just a distant ideal. There is a reason why each person reacts in his own way. And if we knew all the circumstances, we would understand and therefore forgive. We would have a merciful spirit. Jesus said we can not know everything, and so we need to develop a forgiving, understanding attitude anyway.

John Wesley was preaching before General Oglethorpe and was asked to stay for dinner. During the meal, a servant made a blunder. The General banged the table and said, "I never forgive!"

"Then I hope you never sin," Wesley reproached him in a quiet voice, "for to be forgiven, you must forgive."

Are we merciful? Can we pray the Lord's prayer, "Our Father, who art in heaven, . . . Forgive us our trespasses as we forgive those who trespass against us!" Somewhere along there, do we choke?

Queen Victoria and a Mrs. Tullock were in boarding school together as girls. Victoria became queen, the other became the wife of Principal Tullock, a great religious leader. Queen Victoria's husband died and her grief was great. Some weeks later she heard that Principal Tullock had died.

The sympathetic queen came unannounced to the humble school cottage in which the widow lived. When the door was opened and Mrs. Tullock saw Queen Victoria, she started to rise from the bed where she was resting.

The Queen stopped her with a gesture. "I did not come as Queen to subject," she said. "I came as friend to friend."

This is exactly what Jesus did—and much more! He came as man to man, as friend to friend, as brother to brother. He knew our sin, experienced our suffering, and showed us how merciful God is. For the first time men really knew how God loved them.

The world in which we live needs to know how God feels, how He understands us and loves us. One way that others will comprehend His love is through our merciful attitude which reflects it.

Blessed are the pure in heart

Chapter 6

The Privilege of the Pure

A forest ranger in one of our great national parks was somewhat disappointed by a question asked him. In the midst of that outward glory—distant mountains with snow on them, a waterfall, magnificent trees all around, and a coolness that seemed to be sent straight from God—an impatient visitor asked, "Mister, what is there to see around here?"

Uninterested in all the scenery, this man was complaining, evidently wanting programed entertainment. When the ranger did not answer immediately, he repeated his question. "What is there to see around here?"

In disgust, the park ranger finally replied, "Nothing, sir, nothing!"

Though we are surrounded by the beauty of God's world and are recipients of the glory of God's Word, we often ask in frustration, "What is there to see? What is in it for me? Where is the glory of God?" In disappointment, sometimes, the answer has to be, "If you can't see it for yourself, there is nothing!"

The first five beatitudes pointed out how to acquire happiness; the sixth indicates the essence of it. Jesus said, "Blessed are the pure in heart, for they shall see God" (Matthew 5:8). These words immediately imply that we have eyes to see and see not; we have ears to hear and hear not.

The educated eye of the geologist looks at a rock and sees far more than the average person who kicks it out of his path. The trained eye of the astronomer looks up at the sky and sees far more than points of light. An individual who has spiritual sight can see beyond the stars, too—the Bible says that the pure in heart shall see God. Happy is that man who can see God! To be envied are the pure in heart!

Jesus was the Great Physician, and He gives more than just an optical examination. He was not holding a chart in front of His audience and saying, "Can you see these letters, can you see these lines?" For He was not speaking only of our sight, but rather of our insight. There is more for the believer to see, not with his physical eyes, but with his mental, emotional, and spiritual perception.

All around Jesus, the Pharisees and Sadducees were making much of little things. They talked about their ceremonies of cleansing, how they looked after every detail of sacrifice. But inside, Jesus said, they were still unclean, only "whitewashed sepulchres, which indeed appear beautiful outwardly, but are within full of dead men's bones, and of all uncleanness" (Matthew 23:27). And Jesus was talking about spiritual cleanness, about purity of heart. "For man looketh on the outward appearance, but the Lord looketh on the heart" (1 Samuel 16:7).

In the day in which Jesus lived, the people of God came at certain times to offer sacrifices at the altar of the temple. The rich man could buy a lamb without blemish, take it to the priest and say, "Offer it to God for me." The poor man who had nothing to offer and no money to pay could ask for a charity offering and would be provided with a dove. But both of them, the poor man with his dove and the rich man with his lamb, unless they were able to see God in spirit, saw only the priest. If they saw things only through their physical eyes, they missed the glory of God. After all, "Thou shalt love the Lord, thy God, with all thy heart" is the first and greatest commandment (Matthew 22:37–38).

When God was revealing the commandments to Moses, that great lawgiver prayed, "I beseech thee, show me thy glory" (Exodus 33:20).

Whom would you like to see? What would you really like to see? Almost every vacation, every trip is planned with that question in mind—it is either what you want to see or whom you want to see. A loved one, family, a friend? Whom do you want to see? Or, are you going sightseeing? What do you want to see?

Personally, I don't like freeways through towns, even though they can save time. I like to drive slowly and look for the church buildings. I cannot go through a town without wondering, What kind of church do they have here? It tells me something of the character of the town. Of course, I see only the buildings, but they tell me something about the character of the congregation that worships in that meeting house. You can see the church building, also, and not see God.

You can see great wonders of science and not see God. You can see the stars and the mountains and the Grand Canyon—you can see all His creations and not see the Creator. Many people today exhaust themselves traveling around the world to see the great natural and man-made wonders, but how many come into God's house seeking the Creator of body and soul?

Who will really see God when they come to church? Some will see the building, some will see the saints, some will see the sinners—and some will see the mistakes. But only those who seek God will see His majesty.

Of course, even the least of us want occasionally to be a saint—preferably one with a tarnish-free halo that is collapsible and can be conveniently stored away out of sight when it causes any problem between Sundays. But are these words of Jesus an empty promise? Is God waving a "pie in the sky" illusion that man cannot aspire to on earth? Is God offering something man can never experience? Is this promise just another ideal to add to the frustrations? Frustration itself is the result of our inner demand for moral perfection, but it was not meant to produce perpetual guilt. There is a promise of satisfaction to those who wholly seek God.

It often seems incredible that purity of heart could possibly be a reality in our lives. We have to recognize too often that although we may be saints potentially, we are probably sinners presently. Certainly purity of heart is not possible just by wishful thinking—it takes willful living: "Every man that hath this hope in him purifieth himself, even as he [Jesus] is pure" wrote the "Beloved apostle" (1 John 3:3).

We need to remind ourselves that this promise of God is sure and definite, even though the Scriptures tell us that no man shall see God in his time—speaking of our physical eyes. For "God is a Spirit," Jesus said to the woman of Samaria, "and they that worship him must worship him in spirit and in truth" (John 4:24). The pure in heart will see God. Do you desire to see Him?

Prerequisite

The *prerequisite* for seeing God is a pure heart. "Behold, thou desirest truth in the inward parts," said David as he confessed his sin (Psalm 51:6).

What does the word "pure" mean to you? A slogan on a television commercial? In the New Testament the word "pure" is used 28 times. It always means "clean"

—both the Hebrew and Greek words in which our Scriptures were written. We enjoy being clean physically and living in clean surroundings. But could we really enjoy a clean heart?

A man with a pure heart is one with unmixed emotions. His mind, his thoughts, his purposes are unadulterated, unmixed, unconfused. In Matthew 6:22 it says, "If, therefore, thine eye be single, thy whole body shall be full of light." If you have single sight, you are not confused or double-minded. The landscape may be foggy, but you are looking at it clearly. You are focused.

This is what the psalmist meant when he said, "My heart is fixed, O God; my heart is fixed" (Psalm 57:7). The repetition implies a definite commitment, a steady purpose, a firm intent. He was whole-hearted in his dedication.

In the language of the street, to all of us, "pure" is something that hasn't been tampered with. It is free from anything that pollutes it. Gasoline is not pure unless it has been refined; until then it is only raw material. Gold is not "pure gold" until it has been melted and all foreign matter removed. Food is not "pure" food until it has been washed and processed under sterile conditions. Water is not pure water until all contamination and poisonous waste has been removed. If water is impure, you do not purify it at the tap or the hydrant, but at the well. You purify it at the beginning; cleansing is from the source.

To make ourselves better, we can change some outward appearances; we can clean up our "image" on the outside.

The Pharisees were able to do this, but Jesus said that on the inside they were not clean. Just outside washing won't do. There can be no permanent cure of outer symptoms until the inner poison is removed.

The Bible says, "The heart is deceitful above all things, and it is exceedingly perverse and corrupt and severely, mortally sick! Who can know it [perceive, understand, be acquainted with his own heart and mind]?" (Jeremiah 17:9, *Amp*.). Also, "Keep thy heart with all diligence, for out of it are the issues of life" (Proverbs 4:23). All of a man's desires, purposes, and emotions—all he thinks or intends, are governed by his heart. "For as he [a man] thinketh in his heart, so is he" (Proverbs 23:7). This is similar to the expression Jesus used when He said, "The pure in heart shall see God." Obviously, the man with a wicked heart will not see God, but only the one who is pure in heart.

There is in all of us a desperate longing for innocence, a seeking that may be described as part of conscience. It could come from a feeling of guilt or it could be divine conviction. But in most Christians there occurs at some time the fanning of that fire of seeking to know God more perfectly, to see God more clearly. The disciples on the Emmaus Road expressed it when they reported, "Did not our hearts burn within us, while he [Jesus] talked with us along the way?" (Luke 24:32). Surely a pure heart, dominated by love, burning with the words of Jesus, could be a fit home for the perfect God.

In the midst of our sins, failures and frustrations, we

pray desperately for relief. Sometimes in hours spent or misspent, we think of these things and cry out to God. We come to the altar of our own soul and we also come to the meeting house of men with God in deep need.

Provision

Is there provision for our guilt? Is there anything that can make us acceptable to God? "Isn't there some way I can be what God wishes me to be rather than what I am?" So we seek God. We ask God to show Himself to us.

"Create in me a clean heart, O God," the psalmist cried out, "and renew a right spirit within me" (Psalm 51:10). The 23rd chapter of Psalms is familiar to all, but what about the 24th chapter? "Who shall ascend into the hill of the Lord?" it asks, and answers, "He that hath clean hands, and a pure heart" (24:3–4). Who shall see God? Who shall approach His throne? Who shall worship Him in spirit and in truth? The pure in heart. So we pray with David, "Give me a pure heart!"

We need to ask the Great Physician for a clean heart, a new heart, a transplanted heart—a new birth, if you please! The unbeliever can never see God; he hears of God, but he never sees God. Historically, he may know of Jesus, but he does not know Jesus personally as Savior and Lord.

Then is a worship service a secret meeting of the saints? No. But the saints do know somebody others do not know, and they experience something others do not experience. They know God has performed successful cardiac surgery on them. "A new heart also will I give you, and a new spirit will I put within you: and I will take away the stony heart out of your flesh, and I will give you an heart of flesh" (Ezekiel 36:26).

Those who have a clean heart, those who have been born again, those who know God shall hear this of themselves, "These are they . . . [who] have washed their robes, and made them white in the blood of the Lamb" (Revelation 7:14). Purity is an absolute, not a relative condition. *S/S 3. 4* These are God's people because the Lord Jesus has given them a clean heart. For the penitent, the application of the pure, holy blood of Christ.

There is not one of us but what has said at some time, either audibly or in our hearts, "Oh, wouldn't it be wonderful to be as innocent as a little child?" But the promise of a clean heart was not given to unfallen angels, who know nothing of the hurt of sin. This promise was given to the creatures of God who know how sin hurts and who wish to be healed. No man sees God except in judgment —until he wants to.

In our desire to be child-like we say, "Oh, happy is that individual who has never sinned!" But God says, "Blessed is he whose transgression is forgiven, whose sin is covered" (Psalm 32:1). Made whole again? Made like you were? No—better than you ever were. To seek God's face, to experience the new birth, to possess a redeemed heart—this is the greatest happiness. We are con-

verted in order to develop character. Only the redeemed sinner can know how good salvation is and
understand the full love of God.

The communion service is perhaps the most sacred of
our meetings. I think it is because we have a holy hush
on our lips and recognize that we are in the presence of
God. We are reminded by the symbols of what God has
done for us. "Draw nigh unto God," wrote James, "and
he will draw nigh unto you. Cleanse your hands, ye
sinners; and purify your hearts, ye double-minded" (4:8).

In Edinburgh, Scotland, an aged servant of God who
was serving the Lord's Supper noticed that as he passed
the bread a young lady did not take it, and when he passed
the juice she was crying, and shook her head to pass it by.
He knew she had made a profession of faith in the Lord
Jesus and he said, "Take it, Lassie, it's for sinners such as
we." It *is* for sinners such as we! The new birth, the new
heart, the new insight—they are for sinners like us.

Privilege

It is a high *privilege* to see God. "Holy, holy, holy,
Lord God of hosts," chant the angels who guard His
throne.

Someone has well written, "The things which we miss
seeing are really the things which we miss being." We
are part of all we seek after, experience, and comprehend. Poverty-stricken are we if we go day after day,
week after week, miss Sunday after Sunday and never see

God. Many do not see God because their purity has been poisoned and their hearts blinded in their spiritual vision.

The pure in heart will see God—nobody can blind us except our own heart. Oh, to see God! We say sometimes that love is blind. No, love is not blind; it just sees us as we are and loves us anyway. When we love God it is not blindly. We know His holiness and see Him as He is! It is said that Moses "endured, as seeing him who is invisible" (Hebrews 11:27).

To the new Christian I say, "You see God by seeking Him." And those who have been Christians more than a few years should remember that we continue to see God by continuing to seek Him and serve Him. If you are not seeing Him, you need to determine what may be wrong with your spiritual insight. You probably have lost all vision of service to your fellow man, also. Look in your mental attic and clear out everything unchaste, selfish, and unkind.

When do we see God? When we say with Moses, "Show me thy glory." We pray to see His glory when we say with the Lord Jesus Christ, "I do nothing of myself; but as my Father hath taught me . . . I do always those things that please him" (John 8:28–29). When we no longer seek our own glory, our own things, but have singlemindedness toward God, unmixed emotions, an unadulterated heart— our eyes, our aim, our thoughts, our lives fixed on God —we see Him.

When Alfred, Lord Tennyson lay dying, he said to his

103

elder son, whom he had made administrator of his estate, "If my poems are published in a book, see to it that 'Crossing the Bar' is the last poem."

Why? I do not know, unless he wanted to leave in men's minds a last testimony to the fact that his deepest desire was a clearer vision of God.

> I hope to see my Pilot face to face
> When I have crossed the bar.

This is man's last desire, this is man's highest desire. And we see God even here when this becomes our first desire—it is the privilege of the pure!

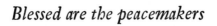
Blessed are the peacemakers

Chapter 7

What the World Wants

What does the world want? It goes without saying we mean, "What does the world want most?"

If you ask a hundred people, probably at least ninety would answer, "Peace!"

When Jesus was speaking on the mountainside, He said, "Blessed are the peacemakers, for they shall be called the children of God" (Matthew 5:9). It seems natural to subscribe to that today, but Jesus' audience must have been shocked by those words.

Perhaps five thousand or more were gathered in that open amphitheater by the lakeside. Evidently a dialogue had taken place prior to Jesus' launching into His main address recorded in the fifth, sixth and seventh chapters of Matthew.

When the great rabbis of the old days wished to teach,

often they would walk informally to and fro. It was commonly accepted that this was an introduction. The teacher was just preparing the ground, just beginning to move toward the important things he had to say. But when the rabbi sat down, it was the cue for sudden quietness. Rapport had been established with the audience and eager minds would be hanging on every word. The men of that day were not degree conscious, but real education was highly prized. Knowledge was desired and wisdom pursued at all costs.

Jesus was counted as a Rabbi and Teacher. "Rabbi, we know that thou art a teacher come from God," Nicodemus greeted Him, "for no man can do these miracles that thou doest, except God be with him" (John 3:2). There was no doubt about it—no other men spoke like this teacher from Galilee.

With an audience there has to be give and take. A man's mind can fasten itself upon words just so long. There must be some relief. Jesus had given several beatitudes, and now He came to one that challenged them, that cut across their deepest emotions. He was talking to people who were strifetorn, subjugated, having a large cancer of hatred eating up their nation's heart.

When they leaned forward to hear Him, Jesus quietly said something that made them recoil: "Blessed are the peacemakers, for they shall be called the children of God."

What strange words of heresy were these? The Jews considered themselves already the children of God, the chosen of God, the nation of God. How could anyone expect them to try to live in peace with the insufferable, iron-heeled Romans? Such concealed but active emotions controlled Jesus' listeners.

When the teacher, the rabbi of those days, sat down, he was saying, to get their attention, "Now, hear this!"

Now I have heard and I still do not understand it. It is one of the most difficult passages of the entire Bible.

Peacemakers? What a paradox! It is in such direct disagreement with our basic human nature.

Dr. Daniel Poling, editor of the *Christian Herald*, made a journey some years ago to North Africa. Our nation was actively engaged in war there and Dr. Poling was with the Chief of Chaplains of the United States Army and the regimental chaplain of that particular battle area. Near the front lines, each evening at a certain time the men who could be spared would gather at the chaplain's headquarters for prayer. This particular night was noisy with bombs bursting and shells shattering.

Nine G. I.'s found their way in the darkness to the little hut, scarcely more than a mud room. The chaplain had prayer and then called on a sergeant to read the lesson. The young soldier began to read from the fifth chapter of Matthew.

When he came to "Blessed are the peacemakers," his voice quivered. He did not read on. "This is a good place to stop," he said. Quietly he picked up his helmet and went back to his post. He had already come to grips with himself and with the issues, with this nation and with his God. The peace he had in his heart was "the peace that passeth all understanding" through the Lord Jesus. He had cast himself in the role of a peacemaker. "We will stop there," he said and went back to the battle for freedom.

The next morning Dr. Poling discovered this young man was from Vermont, "because," he said, "I looked on his dog tags as they carried him away for burial."

What the world craves in our day is peace—peace at any price, many say. Actually, no peace is without price —on the world scene, sometimes it is peace at some nation's price and at the price of many men's lives. There is no peace at pistol point, which is about the only kind the world knows. Often we mistake quietness for peace.

When I was a boy parking cars near a baseball field, I remember the singing of the National Anthem which begins the games. One night, that was just over, when someone stepped to the microphone which could be heard out over the parking area. "We are pleased to announce," he said, "that Chamberlain has reached a cease-fire agreement with Germany." Cheers went up that you could hear all over that part of town. But for days we lived in uneasy quietness. Later we sold extras that declared Germany had surrendered.

Winston Churchill, in Volume Two of his memoirs, said he raised the question with the late President Roosevelt, "What caused World War II?" Finally, the only answer they could agree to was that it was "the unnecessary war." Sometimes it is necessary to wage war to have peace, but the Christian has to recognize that he must wage peace as other men wage war—an all-out effort.

The words Franklin Delano Roosevelt wrote the night before he died were, "We seek peace, enduring peace." Then the pen of the late president lay still.

Our world still seeks peace. We want peace, but we are much like a ship that has been christened, slid down the ways to sail the seven seas, but has a perpetual mutiny on board.

Jesus was talking to Jewish patriots, downtrodden people, poverty-stricken peasants. Perhaps even to some Roman soldiers. He recognized that peace was a difficult thing for men to practice.

Today, many of us have the same emotion as a Frenchman who stood in the Chamber of Deputies when that legislative body was voting to abolish the death sentence in France. Eloquently this Frenchman observed, "I would vote for the abolition of the death penalty, but I wish my friends, the murderers, would vote for it first." He was striking at something basic. There is nothing more fatal than thinking we can do it all by ourselves.

Peacemakers cannot wait for the other part of the world to make peace, however. Ours is not passive compliance, ours is an active effort. It is not the evasion of issues or ignoring of responsibility, but the active facing of things —even when the way is through struggle. "Put on the whole armor of God," is the admonition Paul gave for the Christian soldier. Ours is not an easy battle, this conquest for the minds of men, the souls of men, the peace of mankind.

When Germany blitzed France in World War II, someone later remarked, "London lost its buildings in the war, but Paris, in giving up without a fight, has lost its soul."

Challenge

Jesus was issuing a real *challenge* in this seventh beatitude, or He would not have brought these patriotic, aggressive Jews to the point of high blood pressure. He was talking to men who really wanted to find a leader to bring them victory and freedom. They wanted another warrior-king like David.

Jesus didn't say, "Blessed are the peace lovers." That would take in a lot of people, for most would say, "Oh, I just love peace!" Jesus said, "Blessed are the peace *makers.*"

Need for peace has existed in our world since Adam and Eve declared mutiny against God. Through the ages, cold war has frequently erupted to the boiling point in nations and in men. In our own country today, scarcely a bill goes to a legislature or congress but that new taxes are added, many of them made necessary because men do not live peaceably with one another.

Jesus was asking for more than abolishing argument or disagreement. Is not Russia today trying to eradicate freedom in the minds of men under the guise of peace? "We'll think for you," they declare, "and everyone can agree and live peacefully." Such quietude is slavery. And there is no peace in the hearts of men who are slaves, whether Russian, black, or Israelite. The ancient Jews in captivity mourned, "How shall we sing the Lord's song in a strange land?" (Psalm 137:4).

Two men may argue and one kill the other. Then there will be a strange quietness, for one ceases to speak—but this is not peace. Literature says that Rip Van Winkle and his wife had some stormy sessions around their house. Finally Rip got his musket and walked off, went to sleep, and stayed gone for twenty years. While he took his long nap, there was quietness around the household, but was Mrs. Van Winkle at peace? Quietness is not to be confused with peace.

Many of us do not actually live at peace with one another. One Thanksgiving I asked a member of my club casually, "Are you having a family reunion?"

"I'm not sure whether it is a reunion or just a truce," he retorted. Do we just make truces and go our own way? This is the world crying, "Peace, peace!" when there is no peace. Most of what the world calls peace is only a ragged patchwork quilt.

Character

Jesus spoke of the *character* of peace. "Blessed is the peacemaker!" Such an individual must first find peace in his own heart. No man can be a real peacemaker unless he knows the Prince of Peace. Then he can proclaim God's reconciling word to others.

The qualified peacemaker is one who has faced himself,

has come to grips with his own conflicts. If he has finished his civil war by surrender to Jesus Christ, he is prepared to be an ambassador of peace. Such a man recognizes that much of the bluff he might try on others is a symptom of the noise in his own life, and the man who is constantly at odds with himself is not usually on the square with his fellow man.

After the Kellogg Peace Pact was signed, someone thrust a copy in Senator Kellogg's face before the news microphones of the world and asked, "What can the common man in the street do about peace?" What the senator's concept of Christianity was, I do not know, but he said something very applicable when he answered, "The common man can go across the street and make peace with his neighbor." That is where peace begins.

Jesus was not talking primarily about external peace, but internal peace. It must begin inside; it must begin at home. It is an old saying that "Charity begins at home." Real charity doesn't just stay at home, however, it must overflow. Also the inner peace that is real—when a man comes to peace with himself, he promotes good will without compromise in the world in which he lives. He bridges the gulfs, heals the breaches, and sweetens the bitterness around him.

"What is your concept of perfect peace?" asked an English preacher. "Usually when we want to get away on vacation we go to the high places," he continued, "or to the beach, to somewhere quiet and uncrowded. The men who have the most responsibility often seek a sanc-

tuary where there is no noise, where the hills bec
reminder of God. Perhaps a brook ripples in soothing
silence and the animals come out quietly to drink.

"Why do you call *this* a scene of peace?" the preacher
queried. "Is it not because each one is doing the will of
God for which it was created?"

The same quietude can come inwardly, in our own
world, if the will of God through the Prince of Peace
has been found and followed. Righteousness is the soil
from which peace springs.

An armistice between one nation and another does not
guarantee real peace. A nation may not be at peace within
itself. Prejudice, bitterness, and crime destroy civil peace.
Personal animosities thwart social peace. Even the tongue
can be a terrible weapon. "The tongue can no man
tame," said James; "it is an unruly evil, full of deadly
poison" (3:8). It is not a passive thing.

Abraham Lincoln said, "Whatever they say about me
after I'm gone, may they say this, that I destroy my
enemies by making them my friends." In Christ, God
reconciled the world unto Himself, making enemies into
friends (2 Corinthians 5:19).

General Robert E. Lee, in those terrible days of what
we call the Civil War was bitterly, caustically, nearly in-
humanly criticized by General Whiting. Then at a staff
meeting Jefferson Davis, the Confederate President, asked
General Lee what he thought of General Whiting's quali-
fications for a certain responsibility.

"I believe him to be an officer of unusual capacity,"

replied General Lee, and went on to say several good things about his enemy's ability. Another man called General Lee aside and warned, "You evidently have not heard what General Whiting has been saying about you."

The great Southern General, a great Christian and a great peacemaker, pulled himself erect and said crisply, "O yes, I know. But Mr. Davis did not ask what General Whiting thought of me. He asked me what I thought of General Whiting."

That made a difference. "Blessed are the peacemakers." Why? What is their reward? "For they shall be called the children of God." This is a great honor.

Yes, it began the day we were born again—we became the sons of God. If we are His children, we should be showing the likeness of God. If we are His children, we should be doing God-like work.

Credentials

Peacemaking is a God-like thing. It demonstrates our *credentials* as God's sons.

The Hebrew word for "peace" meant far more than being in comfortable circumstances, undistracted by noise, enjoying untroubled quietness. When the Jews lifted their hands and said, "Peace be unto you and your house," they were saying, "May every good thing in life be yours."

When God speaks peace, He is saying, "You are My children, I know I have already bought you. But the world will know that you are My children by the way you resemble Me. Then they will call you the children of God." Like Father—like son. To be called implies to be owned. If we children are like our Heavenly Father, we will be making an earnest effort to bring all men to the "peace that passeth understanding."

What can the common man, what can the Christian man, what can the average church member do? What can we do at home? What can we do at work? What can we do in other contacts we make every day? Heed the words of Paul when he said, "If it be possible, as much as lieth in you, live peaceably with all men" (Romans 12:18).

Your life will show your credentials, the marks of the prince of Peace, Jesus Christ. "But as many as received him [Jesus] to them gave he power to become the Sons of God" (John 1:12).

How are we going to have peace on earth? We shall never have peace on any block, in any street, in this nation or in the world until spiritual peace is born in human hearts. Peace doesn't come to cities, it comes to individuals.

Every man should like to turn homeward, to his "castle." You sit around in the quietness—or in the noise, it matters little if it is yours or of your making. If you have peace and contentment there, you say there is no place like home. That is external peace, but internal peace is what Jesus gives.

Why do we have the United Nations? Even before that, why was the League of Nations created, although it failed? They were necessary because we haven't recognized that our credentials as Christians consist in going from house to house, person to person, witnessing about the Prince of Peace.

Are you at peace with yourself? Are you at peace with your fellow men? Are you at peace with your God? Would it be a peaceable meeting if you met Him face to face?

"Peace I leave with you, my peace I give unto you," Jesus said to His disciples shortly before His crucifixion. Then one of His first greetings to His disciples after He rose from the dead was, "Peace be unto you?" It was the great gift He had secured for them by death and resurrection.

If we believe that, if we identify ourselves with our Lord, we will take up the role of peacemakers, and people will recognize that we are the children of the God of perfect peace.

> More like the Master I would ever be,
> More of His meekness, more humility;
> More zeal to labor, more courage to be true,
> More consecration for work He bids me do.
> —Charles H. Gabriel

Blessed are they which are persecuted

Chapter 8

The Risk of Righteousness

Jesus concluded the beatitudes recorded in Matthew 5 with a thrust of challenge rather than soothing comfort. Several times He had said, "Happy is that man . . . blessed is that person who reflects the attributes of God." He commended those who would seek meekness, righteousness, mercy, purity, and peace. Then He wrapped up the package with one of the most startling paradoxes in the entire New Testament. He gave them the keys to His kingdom, then warned them what to expect when they dared to unlock the door.

"Blessed are they which are persecuted for righteousness' sake; for theirs is the kingdom of heaven" (Matthew 5:10).

Persecution was not an idle word to His listeners. It wasn't just something they read about in the *Roman Gazette* on Sundays, but a fear they lived with daily. Jesus was saying frankly, "I offer you no bed of roses; I give you no easy path—a cross I share with you." There is a risk to righteousness in this world of conflict.

The people of this world had rather pick flaws than recognize goodness. The devil's crowd will always walk up your back and hound you on every hand. They will set their little traps because they have no desire for higher things. The physician has taken his Hippocratic oath, and the Christian must live with his own commitment. The world is always testing to see whether or not the Christian's is a hypocrite's oath.

A Methodist minister was assigned to a new pastorate in a small town. In a certain business establishment he paid for the things he bought and was given some change. As he closed his fist to put the coins in his pocket, he realized there were four of them, and he thought he should have been given only three. He opened his hand and noticed the change was incorrect.

"You gave me too much money," he said.

"Oh, I knew that," said the merchant. "I was just testing."

Fortunately the minister had enough poise to reply, "Well, are you honest in trying to trap me? I'd rather deal with someone I can trust to be fair."

The world is always looking for flaws and failures. The righteous are constantly on trial. It may not be in court and it may not be with a psychological lie detector, but you will be tested. It may be in different areas they try to probe to see if you ring true. For the world has had its fill of counterfeits, imitations, facsimiles, and substitutes. They are hunting for the real thing.

It is tragic that the world tests us with sly trickery, always trying to trap someone in the wrong. But there is a secret hope, an inner desire, a searching on the part of that man who watches critically. Somehow aware of his own emptiness, he is looking for something real, whether he realizes it or not. He is trying to say, "Is there somebody who has a sense of values, who can be trusted, who is genuine?" Even though some, with laughter, try to back a man down from his ethics and from his Christian principles, secretly they are hoping he will stand true. They are looking for somebody to show them the way.

Persecution

Or else, out of their own evil and frustration, they will persecute him. *Persecution* is a word that strikes us with horror. We have never lived in a land that has known political persecution, and we have seen very little evidence of religious persecution. Most of us do not comprehend the sacrifices of the New Testament Christians. When we talk about persecution, it is as if our mind shifts into another world and says, "What savagery! Today we are too civilized for that!"

Several years ago I interviewed a young man for a staff position in our church. He was a music student in a nearby university and was interested in being a symphony director. I tried to deal with him on middle ground over a meal together. Because of his background, our discussion included the subject of religious persecution. "My mother and I lived on grass for days, one time," he confided, "without bread at all." It is hard to imagine such a thing in our land.

In the New Testament, slanderous statements were made against the churches. For one thing, they were accused of heresy and blasphemy. Their world had its many gods and little understanding of the One God. For most of the first century, the Christians did not have much access to the written epistles to read in their gatherings. There were no printed pages, no Gospels of John that could be passed out on the street corner. They had simply heard the words of evangelists and Christians from Jerusalem.

Outsiders heard rumors that when the Christians sat down to take the Lord's Supper they quoted, "This is my body"—and they considered this cannibalism. All it takes to make a rumor fact to some people is, "Well, I heard it that way!"

The people of that day did not recognize the spiritual implications of what Jesus had said to His disciples—words that the Christians were repeating in memory of their Lord Jesus Christ. Don't say it doesn't make any difference what we believe! Men have died for the privilege of gathering together at the Lord's Table.

Also, outsiders completely misunderstood what Chris-

The Risk of Righteousness

tains called their "Love Feast" where they talked about being brothers and sisters in Christ. This was an alien thing in a world that had a completely selfish attitude: "It's all for me and mine!" And they couldn't understand those who cared about anybody else. So they attached to the Christian "Love Feast" other connotations, as evil men always do.

Fierce fires of persecution were turned loose on the early church less than a hundred years from the time Jesus spoke His Sermon on the Mount. It was said concerning the Christian church that they were a group of radical reactionaries. "Every group is a cell of criminals," they said about them.

Why? Because for these early Christians the things of this life seemed to have lost their attraction. They did not talk about mansions here, but about the fact that Jesus was coming again. They said that when He comes this old world will be destroyed. The Christians were called subversives and thought to be trying to destroy the Roman Empire because they believed in the return of Christ. The proud Romans thought their world would never end. They persecuted the Christians for their religious doctrines.

These were the bases of public persecution, but there was an abundance of persecution that was more personal. Many conflicts arose over ethics—one man's relationship with another. This is probably the area in which you and I will be tested in our time—our loyalties.

What does being a Christian mean to you? If you heard

that persecution was coming to your church, what would you do? Would you desert it and say, "I'm not going back until it is over; I don't want to be involved"? Jesus never took the detached approach. He came down into this world and was deeply involved.

In the early church, the Christians were involved whether they wished to be or not. If one was a brick mason, for instance, he might be employed in building a temple to a pagan god. He was faced with a choice concerning his Christian convictions. Can a Christian build the altar on which a pagan god is going to be worshiped with sacrifices?

Another problem early Christians faced was the effect on their social life. Usually only a small portion of the heathen offering was put on the altar. A portion was given to the priest for his upkeep and the idol temple. Then the rest was used at a feast, a banquet. They would say to Christian neighbors, "Come and eat with us." But Christ was very real to these Christians and it was hard to swallow meat that had been offered to pagan idols.

Instead of a Christian grace, their pagan neighbors would make a salute to the gods of Rome. If you believe in Christ, are you going to tip your glass to the pagan gods of Rome?

But the greatest handicap for the Christian was political. Many non-Romans acquiesed easily to Roman rule because the Romans at least chased out the pirates, enforced criminal laws, and kept civil peace. But the Romans began to think they owned the world. They increased taxes fantastically. "Great is Rome!" they declared. Everything important develops an identity symbol, and the emperor became the personification of Roman greatness. Astute politicians promoted emperor worship as a way of unifying the Empire.

"Are you for Christ or Caesar?" became a pressing question for every man. Christians went along, trying to be inconspicuous, avoiding the worship of Caesar in public places and worshipping Christ in their homes or in the catacombs or wherever else they might find privacy. But there came a day when everybody had to report for the poll tax, to secure a "certificate of liberty." In receiving this certificate, a man had to say, "I pledge my allegiance to Caesar as supreme Lord." The Christians did not wish to pay homage to Caesar, so they were in for trouble.

Jesus had told them long before that they were going out into a pagan world. In the actualities of life, every situation in which you find yourself will not open with prayer and close with a benediction in the glow of sunshine through stained-glass windows. The Christians were truly as lambs among wolves.

Purpose

Yes, there is a risk to righteousness. Loyalty to God takes a firm *purpose*. You have to be willing to face the dangers. The suffering of the early Christians showed their great love for Christ. The Roman Empire was weakened by its persecuting this underground movement of those who loved Christ more than they loved their own lives.

Polycarp, the Bishop of Smyrna in the first century, was told, "All you have to do is renounce this Jesus and you shall have your life spared."

"No, I will not," Polycarp said. "Eighty and six years have I served Christ and He has never wronged me or failed me." Then he bowed his head and prayed, "O God, I thank Thee that Thou hast counted me worthy for this hour." The great and faithful bishop preached his most effective sermon in the arena that day. He showed his loyalty to Christ—even at the cost of suffering and death.

Jesus said, "Blessed are ye, when men shall revile you, and persecute you, and shall say all manner of evil against you falsely, for my sake. Rejoice, and be exceeding glad; for great is your reward in heaven" (Matthew 5:11–12).

A song writer declared, "Brethren, we are treading where the saints have trod." Those who suffer have made it easier for those who come after.

This is also true in our time. At Boulder Dam there is a plaque upon which are listed the names of the men who died taming that wilderness and building that great reservoir for water. The memorial declares of them, "These have made the desert to blossom like a rose." Many things are easier in our time because somebody else has sacrificed.

In London, almost a century ago, George Adam Smith met a young man of his acquaintance on the street and asked, "Where have you been?"

"I have been to see my mother for the last time," the young man replied.

"Why do you say, 'for the last time'? You ar‹
thirty years old."

"Because I am going to the Congo tomorrow, and I'm
not blind to the fact that the average life of a missionary
in the Congo [that was in the 1800's] is less than two and
a half years." Such consecration and self-denial has not
been the exception among those who love the Lord.

The Christian's life must be ruled by a purpose different
from that which motivates others. This is revealed by a
story found in *The Evangel.* "A writer for a great news-
paper once visited India. While there he met a missionary
nurse who lived among the lepers and ministered to their
need. He noticed how tender and loving she was to those
poor souls. Looking at her in amazement, the reporter
commented, 'I wouldn't wash their wounds for a million
dollars!'

" 'Neither would I,' said the Christian worker, 'but I
gladly do it for my Savior. The only reward I'm looking
for is His smile of approval.' "

She had found a real purpose in life, because her life
was controlled by the desire to hear Him say, "Well done,
thou good and faithful servant."

Pattern

Christianity has been a *pattern* of persecution, sacrifice,
problems in ethics—living in our world and living with
ourselves. It is a strange religion that offers both a Cross

and a Comforter. But in a world filled with great wrong, that is where the righteous belong.

A popular song of some years ago said,

> We'll build a little nest somewhere out in the West,
> And let the rest of the world go by.

Jesus did not just "let the rest of the world go by," and that is not His plan for us. In His great high priestly prayer to His Father, Jesus said, "I pray not that thou shouldest take them out of the world, but that thou shouldest keep them from the evil" (John 17:15).

Jeremiah wept over God's sinning people and cried out, "Oh, that I might let the people go!"—that is, let them have their own way without the cost of warning them and grieving over them. But he could not. He recognized the pattern of the people of God.

What is that pattern? "We are troubled on every side," said Paul, "yet not distressed; we are perplexed, but not in despair; Persecuted, but not forsaken; cast down, but not destroyed" (2 Corinthians 4:8–9).

"If the world hate you," Jesus said, "you know that it hated me before it hated you." Then He reminded them, "The servant is not greater than his lord" (John 15:18, 20).

It has been said that every historian writing about the progress of the Christian faith has declared that "the blood of the martyrs is the seed of the church." You ask me why there is no harvest today? Perhaps because there has been no seed sown.

A certain Christian young man was preparing to go to a

lumber camp. He was warned by friends that it would be very difficult to be a Christian in such a place. The men were rough and would deride and scoff at the things of the Lord and make life miserable for one professing faith in Christ.

When he returned, his friends asked, "How did you manage to get along with that godless crowd?"

"Oh, I got along fine!" he answered. "They never caught on that I was a Christian."

That is not the correct pattern for the truly Christian life. Our witness is to shine forth in spite of whatever trouble it might cause us.

For those who dare the fire of persecution, God promises His presence. Nebuchadnezzar looked into that fiery furnace and said, "Did not we cast three men, bound, into the midst of the fire? . . . Lo, I see four men loose, walking in the midst of the fire, and they have no hurt; and the form of the fourth is like the Son of God" (Daniel 3:24–25). Jesus had not been born in human flesh, yet this pagan ruler said the fourth man looked like the Son of God.

Today the world is still testing God's children. And to be sure they get results, they surely heat the furnace seven times hotter. Jesus never said things wouldn't be hard for us. He didn't say our path wouldn't get difficult, He didn't say our surroundings wouldn't be desolate, He didn't say our circumstances wouldn't seem discouraging. He never said it would be easy, but He said it would be exciting.

Abel suffered because he made an acceptable offering to God. People will criticize the man who is trying to offer himself. The person who isn't making it will find ways to cut down and criticize.

David is pursued by Saul, John the Baptist was beheaded, Jesus crucified. They took the risk of the righteous. Do you dare follow them?

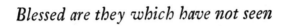

Blessed are they which have not seen

Chapter 9

Sight Unseen

In addition to the eight beatitudes quoted in Matthew 5, two other beatitudes spoken by Jesus are mentioned in the New Testament. The one in John 20:29 is perhaps as well known as any other of the sayings of Jesus: "Blessed are they that have not seen, and yet have believed."

All the beatitudes in the fifth chapter of Matthew were spoken during Jesus' early, and therefore pre-resurrection ministry. This one recorded in John is from post-resurrection time. It came after Jesus' miracle-filled ministry, vicarious death, and victorious resurrection. Every Christian ought to listen intently when Jesus says, "blessed," for He is talking about things which are our great legacy as Christians. This is that state of heaven on earth that

God shares with us now—and He has promised even more.

The city of the King, Jesusalem, has been overrun by its enemies many times. Each conqueror who succeeded in occupying the outlying territories immediately began his journey toward the capital city on the mountains. It was the center of religious observance, and this inflamed the desire of many dictators.

One military general, as soon as he crushed Jerusalem, went into the Temple and pulled back the sacred curtain. It has been his secret desire to see the Holy of Holies, of which he had heard the tradition of the Hebrews that it was the holy place of their God. Being a pagan, he expected to find great riches such as surrounded pagan idols. There would be costly and beautiful things for him to behold and he would plunder what he found.

This place was sanctified by the presence of the Creator-God and was regarded as unimaginably holy by the people who worshiped there. When the pagan general entered the Temple with heavy boots and a thoughtless mind, he was disappointed to find nothing behind the curtain that he could gaze upon—no relics, no gold, no diamonds.

Standing in the Holy of Holies, the place where God dwelt, this general looked for the gold of man. He missed completely the glory of God.

This is not unusual. Many men come into the house of God with heavy boots and pagan hearts, trample on the holy things of God, and are far more interested in counting the offering than they are in the fact that the glory of God could fill them.

Do we miss God? Do we miss seeing His glory? Do we have eyes only for those things that distract? If so, then we leave God's house as disappointed as was that pagan of another day.

When Moses came upon the burning bush, he recognized that God was speaking to him. A man with a timid soul and a stammering tongue, Moses had difficulty adjusting himself to the challenges God gave him. But he was never the same after he had seen the glory of God and heard the voice of God. When we come, in New Testament fashion, to behold the glory of Christ, when we recognize that He died on Calvary, when we understand His precious sacrifice, then we ought never to be the same.

But sometimes a man sees only the historical Jesus and never the personal Jesus.

Many times a school teacher sits down at the desk with a pupil and explains the problem at hand. Often the child will say, as you and I have said, "I see," when we really didn't see. We just knew that it was expected of us. Perhaps we were afraid that her continuing attention might embarrass us. The problem today is that many people do not have a personal, "original" experience with God. They perceive nothing more than faded carbon copies, but say, "I see," when really they have not beheld for themselves the glory of God.

After Thomas saw for himself the nail prints in the

hands of the Savior, his doubts were dispelled. When we meet Jesus today, though we do not behold him with our physical eyes, we can see Him with the eyes of faith.

On a street corner, I passed a blind man playing a guitar. His music was really not appealing and it seemed a pitiful sight. But I caught a phrase that had particular meaning. He was singing—much the way I sing, off-key— "At the cross, at the cross, where I first saw the light . . ." As we each approach the cross, blinded by the things of this life, it is only there that we can first see the light, when we see Jesus by faith.

Just before a Sunday evening preaching service, D. L. Moody was asked by a man if he would grant an interview during the following week. The man had three questions to ask. Because in that church people came from as much as thirty miles, Mr. Moody and the man selected the hour prior to the Wednesday evening service.

But in that Sunday night service, the man came, with repentance toward God, to faith in the Lord Jesus Christ. On Wednesday the man did not show up. At the prayer service, Mr. Moody noticed the man's radiant face and sought him out. "I had an appointment with you," he said, "but you didn't keep it. You said you had some questions to ask me."

"Mr. Moody," the man replied, "when by faith I accepted Jesus Christ as my Savior Sunday night, He took me at face value and I took Him by faith, sight unseen. All the questions in my mind vanished."

Reproved Faithlessness

Jesus' doubting disciple, Thomas, had some problems. The Master exhorted him, "Be not faithless, but believing" (John 20:27). Here Jesus *reproved faithlessness*. The preacher who tries to help people has to help men with their doubts. As that great prince of preachers, Charles Haddon Spurgeon, advised, "Don't try to answer a man's questions, seek to answer his needs."

Thomas was nicknamed "Didymas," meaning "twin." If he had a twin we are not told, specifically, we only know this word means "twin." Did he have a twin unknown to us? That is altogether possible, for the New Testament does not say a great deal about genealogy— except that of Jesus. It is far more concerned with the brothers and sisters in Christ's fellowship. The name "Didymas" may have come from the fact that the others saw in Thomas a man who was really two persons. He could descend to deep depths and go to vast heights.

You remember the occasion when Jesus said that He was going to Jerusalem, after He got the message that Lazarus was very ill. His disciples, alarmed, remonstrated, "Master, if you go to Jerusalem they will surely kill you." But Jesus steadfastly set His face toward Jerusalem.

Thomas spoke up and said, "Let us also go, that we may die with him!" (John 11:16).

In the next place we find Thomas quoted, he was asking a question. In the 14th chapter of John, Jesus was telling

His disciples that He was going away, but He would return for them: "Whither I go ye know, and the way ye know."

Thomas spoke up quickly. "Lord, we know not whither thou goest, and how can we know the way?" (John 14:5).

This disciple will always be remembered, rightly or not so rightly, for his denseness and doubts. That is what we think of first when we think of Thomas, just as we think of denial when we think of Simon Peter and of wistful questions when we think of Pilate. In one crucial hour of life, these men did something that went down in history as the thing people remember them by.

It may not be pleasant for us to realize that people probably will not remember us by a lifetime of action. They will usually remember us by one thing, if they remember us at all. But if, after we pass from the stage of this life, people remember one good thing, we will have made significant contribution to our society and to our world.

We do not scold Thomas for honest questions. Rather, we suffer with him for the difficulties that he had, because faith never comes easy. It was always a problem to Thomas. Did his doubts arise out of his mind or out of his disposition? Was he by nature a pessimist who was able to see just the bad things, as some people do?

Perhaps. The apostles were men of like passions as we are, and there seem to be many people with this doubting nature. They can see all the things that are wrong before they are able to grasp anything that is right. Thomas was always skeptical, always curious, always cautious. But to Thomas' credit it must be said that he was forever loyal, and this cannot be said of all of us.

I still marvel at the patience of the Savior, who let a man dictate his own terms of belief. Thomas was challenging the Triune God when he declared, "I will not believe until I see!" What right did Thomas have to touch those slightly healed wounds in Jesus' hands? Only the right that Jesus gave to him. "I'll not believe," he said, "until I'm able to test for myself.

Renewed Fellowship

Jesus not only reproved Thomas' faithlessness, but He brought him into *renewed fellowship*. Thomas was not with the other disciples when Jesus came the first time after His resurrection. That tells us a lot. Absenteeism leads to doubt. And, of course, you cannot get anything out of worship if you do not come. When a person does not worship, he gets away from God, and when he gets away from God, he gets out of the center of things. It's not far from spiritual sins to carnal sins—not a long step.

There is a habit which I call "the preacher's sport," where they take advantage of the people who are present to harangue those who are absent. I gave that up a long time ago, because I think it only fair that the people who come get something for their effort. Nevertheless, absenteeism was part of the failure of Thomas and it is the blight of the Christian church today.

Thomas was not with them when Jesus came. The disciples were not holding a revival in which they expected great results. They were not in a service when "Heaven came down and glory filled my soul." They were not around when there were those who needed to be visited. They were not around when those who were hungry needed to be fed.

Judas was not with them and nobody thought anything about it, for Judas had departed and gone to his own place. Pilate was not with them; he had already asked all the questions and gotten all the answers that he wanted. Caiaphas. the high priest, was not there when Jesus came; the soldiers were not there and nobody thought anything about it. But the disciples did feel that Thomas should have been there. How can we be part of the fellowship if we are not fellowshipping?

But Thomas came into renewed fellowship. He came back to say, "My Lord and my God!"

He had been out yonder in solitary confinement, but not eating that living bread and drinking that living water Jesus had provided. He was feeding himself on the disillusionment of what he had seen. Thomas was grieving, like the disciples on the road to Emmaus whom Jesus reproached for their pessimism: "O foolish ones, and slow of heart to believe!" (Luke 24:25). Thomas was slow of heart, and, like them, foolish. It is a foolish thing not to believe in Jesus.

A tragic thing happened on the streets of London in recent years. A blind man stood at a corner and held out his hand. Usually someone would take his hand and guide him across the street. Just as he lifted up his left hand, another hand touched it. He thought it was a safe hand and they started out into the street together, only to be run down by the traffic. When the two men were carried to the hospital, it was discovered that both of them were blind, and each was reaching out for help—but they could not help each other.

There are many who are blind and cannot see, deaf and cannot hear. And "There is a way which seemeth right unto a man, but the end thereof are the ways of death" (Proverbs 14:12). Many reach out a hand to someone for help, and if those who have spiritual insight do not take that hand, someone else will lead them to destruction.

If Thomas didn't believe in Jesus, if he could not say, "My faith looks up to Thee, Thou Lamb of Calvary," how could he expect to have any message? He didn't have. If he didn't believe, how could he expect others to believe him? If you don't believe what you teach, how will you teach others?

Robust Faith

From this experience there came into the life of Thomas a *robust faith*. He was slow to believe, but finally he made a complete surrender when he exclaimed, "My Lord and my God!"

As Pascal said, "The heart has its reasons, that reason cannot know." Thomas' heart responded when the turmoil of his reason was stilled.

John came to know Jesus with a logical mind; Mary Magdalene came to know Jesus with a hungry heart; but Thomas came to know Jesus only with a surrender of his will: "The word is nigh thee," Paul quoted in Romans 10:8, and it had been nigh Thomas all the time.

The captain of a large ship set sail from Liverpool, bound for New York, with his family among those on board. One night a sudden squall arose, struck the vessel and almost capsized it. Everything movable was sent tumbling and everyone was alarmed. Many sprang from their berths and began to dress.

The captain's eight-year-old daughter awakened with fright. When she was told about the severe storm, she asked, "Is Father on deck?" Assured that he was, she dropped back on her pillow without fear and was soon fast asleep in spite of the storm.

The child had confident faith in her father and in his ability to protect and provide for her. How much more should we Christians exhibit such faith in our heavenly Father!

Thomas learned confident faith in his Lord. We have to admit he was no ready-made saint. He spurned a second-hand creed and fought his way through doubt, his Lord bringing him to victory.

Tradition has it that Thomas went to India as one of the first foreign missionaries and ended his life there, a faithful servant of the Lord Jesus who planted a church which has endured through the centuries. Certainly his own bold testimony as a convinced doubter would have had great impact on those who worshipped dead idols or dead philosophers.

For those who through the centuries have believed in Jesus Christ though they have not seen Him, God has a special blessing. "Come, ye blessed of my Father," Jesus said, "inherit the kingdom prepared for you from the foundation of the world" (Matthew 25:34).

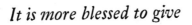

It is more blessed to give

Chapter 10

Declared
Divine Dividends

We can never cover all the beatitudes in the Bible, for there are at least a hundred passages where blessings are declared. But as a coda to the beatitudes spoken by Jesus on the Mount, let us add one we find in Acts 20:35: "It is more blessed to give than to receive."

Jesus used eight "Blessed . . ." statements in His Sermon on the Mount, which we refer to as "the Beatitudes." These were pre-resurrection beatitudes. Then there was the one that takes on unusual emphasis from the fact that Jesus said it after His resurrection. We marvel at His patience and wonderful love as He answered Thomas' doubts: "Blessed are they that have not seen, and yet have believed" (John 20:29).

Now we come to a beatitude that we have to call a "rumored remark." I do not use the word "rumor" lightly, as though it were an untruth, for Paul was speaking. He was talking with elders from the church at Ephesus, and he knew it was probably the last time he would see them. He also knew that in a short time they would face persecution; they would have to take a sacrificial stand for Jesus Christ. Tribulation such as they had not previously experienced would engulf their lives. Therefore Paul was encouraging them not to think of themselves, but of others.

It may have been in the darkness of night that these Ephesian church leaders took Paul down to the oceanside with tearful good-byes and pushed him off in a boat. But whatever the conditions of that last meeting, this word from Paul was emphatic: "I have shown you all things, . . . and to remember the words of the Lord Jesus, how he said, It is more blessed to give than to receive" (Acts 20:35).

How did Paul know that Jesus said this? It is not recorded in the gospels, but in the 20th chapter of John we read, "And many other signs truly did Jesus . . . which are not written in this book," and "even the world itself could not contain the books that should be written" (21:25).

Where, then, did this beatitude come from? Probably by word of mouth down through the years. Over and over again the saying must have been passed on, "It is more blessed to give than to receive—Jesus said that!"

It may have been—and I presume here—that this was

spoken by Jesus when the little boy gave his five loaves and two fishes to feed the multitude. The little fellow's eyes became large with enthusiasm as he saw his sack lunch being blessed. An impressive group of men lined up, and Jesus multiplied with His blessing this little lunch. The boy never was the same because of what he saw that day by the Sea of Galilee. It may have been that he spent his life saying to everyone, "Jesus said it is more blessed to give than to receive! It was better for me to give my lunch to Jesus than to eat it."

It may have been that Jesus' words were spoken when He saw that poor woman in the Temple putting into the treasury all that she had—only two mites. "It is more blessed to give than to receive."

Another woman gave a great deal when she broke an alabaster box of ointment on Jesus' head. "Wherever this gospel shall be preached throughout the whole world," He said, "this also that she hath done shall be spoken of, for a memorial of her." For her, indeed, it was more blessed to give.

These were haunting words among the words that were heralded to the church, for the words of Jesus passed on by those who heard Him kept the early church alive. This was the declared, divine dividend for divine generosity.

Measure of Giving

There are some things that are not debatable. It *is* more blessed to give than to receive! God said that you will receive in the same proportion that you give—in the spirit and manner in which you give. Will your *measure of giving* be stingy, or shaken down and yet overflowing? If you take in everything and give out nothing, you become sterile as the Dead Sea. You have to give to live.

"God is love," Henry Drummond said, "and giving is the language of love—there is no other common language on the face of the earth among men." Money is cheap if you cannot buy, and tomorrow has no days.

In the well-written novel called *Three Came Home*, based on historical fact, the scene was a prison camp. The men prisoners were kept in one place, the women in another, and there was a separate place for the children.

Even though the condition of the children was pitiful—a thing revolting to all of us in a humane society—at least they were better off than the women, and the womens' conditions were much better than the mens'. But the need to give stirred among the men one day. They made up an offering of about $50 and, through the Red Cross, sent it to the women with the request that it should be used for the children.

The women, knowing the terrible conditions under which the men had to live, many of them battered and sick, reasoned, "Our plight is better than theirs, and the children get even better care. Shouldn't we send the money back and ask the men to use it for themselves?"

One wife, an older woman, raised the question, "Do you want to take away their manhood, their strength, their will to live? This proves they are men instead of animals. If you give it back to them, and do not use it for the comfort of the children, you take away their strength to sacrifice."

There is something about us that makes it necessary for us to do something for others. If we are not allowed to be generous, if that privilege is taken away from us, much of the joy of living is lost.

"It is more blessed to give than to receive" is a truth that goes far beyond almsgiving or personal gifts. It includes one's contribution to the community and to the world.

Many years ago in the city of Athens a large group waited for news of the outcome of a sea battle between the Greeks and the Persians which was taking place some 25 miles offshore. Their lives and their hopes hung in the balance. Would they be victors or victims when the battle was over? This was a decisive conflict, a turning point of history.

After the Greeks had waited a long, anxious time, their nerves on edge, worry growing into pessimism, a runner came into sight. With a last burst of strength, he threw himself in front of the leader. He was able to gasp only one word, "Victory!" Then he collapsed, dead. With his last strength he had run his last mile.

This noble deed was taken out of its setting to make a contemporary point in the *Saturday Review:* they told it that during an invasion, a runner came to those waiting for news, sank to the ground, and with a blank expression gasped, "I forgot! I forgot the message!"

In churchly sanctuaries, singing familiar hymns, people still wait anxiously for the glorious gospel of Good News. Sometimes, in a cartoon setting, with the world poking fun—because in some cases our strength is gone—we stand as if saying, half-apologetically, "I forget! I don't remember the message I was commissioned to deliver!"

"It is more blessed to give than to receive!" Cynics ask, Is this what Jesus really said? Or is it just one of those proverbs that men pass along and it gets better with time? Do you think Jesus really meant it? You have to decide, for this is a way of life. How you feel about this affects your emotions and is vitally connected with your entire philosophy of life. It determines whether you try to get all you can and keep it, or whether you are willing to submit yourself to Jesus' way of serving all that you can and doing it with supreme joy.

In school, children are encouraged to make something to take home. Although it may be a paper covered with wobbly strokes of a loose crayon, when he presents his work, it should be received as an immortal work of art. From your face and your eyes the child seeks direction and encouragement, being taught by your reactions. There is nothing children sense more quickly than their parents' attitude about giving to God.

A wise mother asked her twelve-year-old girl to take some flowers, which the mother cut from her garden, to a sick woman down the street. The child came back skipping and smiling and started into the house to wash her hands. The mother said, "Smell your hands before you wash them." Of course, she could still smell the flowers.

"Always remember," the mother said, "that the fragrance of what you give away stays with you." The girl's hands, having held the gift of flowers, retained the fragrance, a treasure they would not have had if the flowers had remained in the garden, uncut and ungiven.

Have you received this beatitude? Do you experience the lingering fragrance of giving? It is a financial beatitude, yes, but an unselfish beatitude and the supreme beatitude. Have you ever opened your heart to it?

Measure of Receiving

There is another idea implied here, the *measure of receiving*. God made us with free will, and it is possible for us not to receive, but to reject. In this materially-oriented society, rejection of a gift is a very uncommon thing. In this "welfare world" it sometimes seems that everybody has his hand out. In the spiritual realm it is quite different. Many people reject God as unnecessary and think they can manage on their own. Yet it is He who "giveth us richly all things to enjoy" (1 Timothy 6:17).

Most of us enjoy good health, for instance. That is a gift from God, because over many of our physical ailments we seem to have little control.

To lose one's eyesight suddenly and have to depend upon someone else for a guiding hand would not be a very happy situation, but it would be good to receive help. We are used to getting out of bed and moving around easily and almost automatically. Walking unassisted, we do not realize how good it might be, if we were handicapped, to have someone to depend on to help us. There is nothing wrong with receiving, but under any condition, it is better to be in a position to give than to have to receive help.

We all like to receive, and it is a special characteristic of childhood. Every parent knows this. When you give something to a child, your own or someone else's, you see the wide-eyed expression—and there are various ways of saying, "Thank you!" You see their little world of wonder open up before you, and you have to say, "This is good, this is very beautiful!"

Certainly there is nothing wrong with receiving. We are told to receive from God and that all our blessings come from Him in the first place. It is on that basis that we are to give: "Freely ye have received, freely give" (Matthew 10:8).

An Englishman named Hyde, very deeply in debt, suddenly realized that he owed his greatest debt to God. He immediately began paying God first—although he had wondered if it might be dishonest to give the Lord His portion while he was still obligated to human creditors. After all, the Bible also said, "Owe no man anything."

Eventually, Mr. Hyde was able to reimburse all his other creditors in full. The Lord blessed him for his liberality according to Proverbs 11:25: "The liberal soul shall be made fat, and he that watereth shall be watered also himself." Mr. Hyde later became a wealthy man.

Jesus gave liberally of Himself. He kept the very strict laws of the Mosaic Code, including tithing. Any time He broke the smallest of their laws, even healing a man with a withered hand on the Sabbath, He was severely criticized by the Jewish leaders. If He had not kept the requirement of tithing, they would have set after Him like hungry wolves.

There is nothing people think of more quickly than money; it was the one thing in which Jesus' enemies would have been glad to trap Him. But He gave. Other men reject the principle of consistent giving to God. If they miss that week and that month, it is over with and they have no more responsibility. They feel that if they are not there for the show, they owe no admittance.

A Christian accountant took the whole question of giving and receiving very seriously and decided to keep a daily balance sheet. On one side he listed all he did for God; on the other, all the Lord did for Him. If some small need was met by God's gracious hand, he put that down. All God's favors and mercies were recorded. After a few weeks of this bookkeeping, the man gave up. "It's no use," he said, "I can never get ahead. I am always hopelessly in debt."

God often tries us with a little to see what we will do with a lot. We cannot outgive Him.

Measure of Reward

"It is more blessed to give than to receive" is not a contrast but a comparison. It implies an abundant *measure of reward*. Jesus was saying, "Walk with Me, come with Me to the very heights, to the joy of giving in a sublime manner, in complete surrender to God."

Some of God's humble saints seem to practice giving in spite of their own apparent need. Like the widow of Zarephath in 1 Kings 17, who fed Elisha out of her dwindled supply, they find that their "cruse of oil" does not fail nor the "barrel of meal" diminish. Somehow God replenishes their supply from unexpected sources.

Yet from our churches we often have a strange silence concerning giving; it is almost non-existent in our Bible lessons, in our teaching and preaching. More Christian lives seem to get wrecked in this realm than anywhere else, because all their attitudes toward the things of God are affected.

In the temple, Christ called attention to the poor woman who gave her two mites. She did not know she was being observed. Sometimes we create distractions, hoping God will not be watching the collection plate. "Giving" is not a dirty word, it is a divine word, a declared dividend: "It is more blessed to give than to receive."

Many years ago a young girl, hearing a missionary in deep need make an earnest plea for support, came forward with more than four dollars—back when that was more than fourteen dollars would be now.

"How did you collect so much, Mary?" she was asked. "You're so young!"

"I earned it," the girl replied. "When I thought how Jesus died for me, I wanted to do something for Him. I made that $4.32 by collecting rain in pails and selling the soft water for two cents a bucket."

Giving should be done with rejoicing, according to the apostle Paul in 2 Corinthians 9:7, "for God loveth a cheerful giver." This makes giving a Christian grace, and it applies to more than money.

A prominent Englishman of the 19th century was returning after an extended stay in India. His aged mother could not go to the station to meet him, but sent a carriage and driver. The man asked her how he could recognize her son.

"Look for a man who is helping someone else," she replied.

Following her advice, the driver carefully observed the people as they left the train. Before long he noticed a gentleman assisting an elderly lady to the platform, then carrying out her luggage. Approaching him, the coachman found he was the distinguished statesman he had been sent to meet.

"Look not every man on his own things," wrote the apostle Paul, "but every man also on the things of others" (Philippians 2:4). When we forget ourselves in meekness and mourning, mercy and peacemaking, faithfulness and liberality, we do those things which add true beauty to our lives here and hereafter.

Jesus summarized the Beatitudes in His Sermon on the Mount, a few verses later, with a simple exhortation and a forecast of its end result which is, as one creed states it, "the chief end of man." It is a well-known but little followed verse: "Let your light so shine before men, that they may see your good works and glorify your father, who is in heaven" (Matthew 5:16).